The

PLEASURE OF GARDENING

DESIGNING THE CONTAINED GARDEN

Inspirational ideas for
patios, courtyards and containers

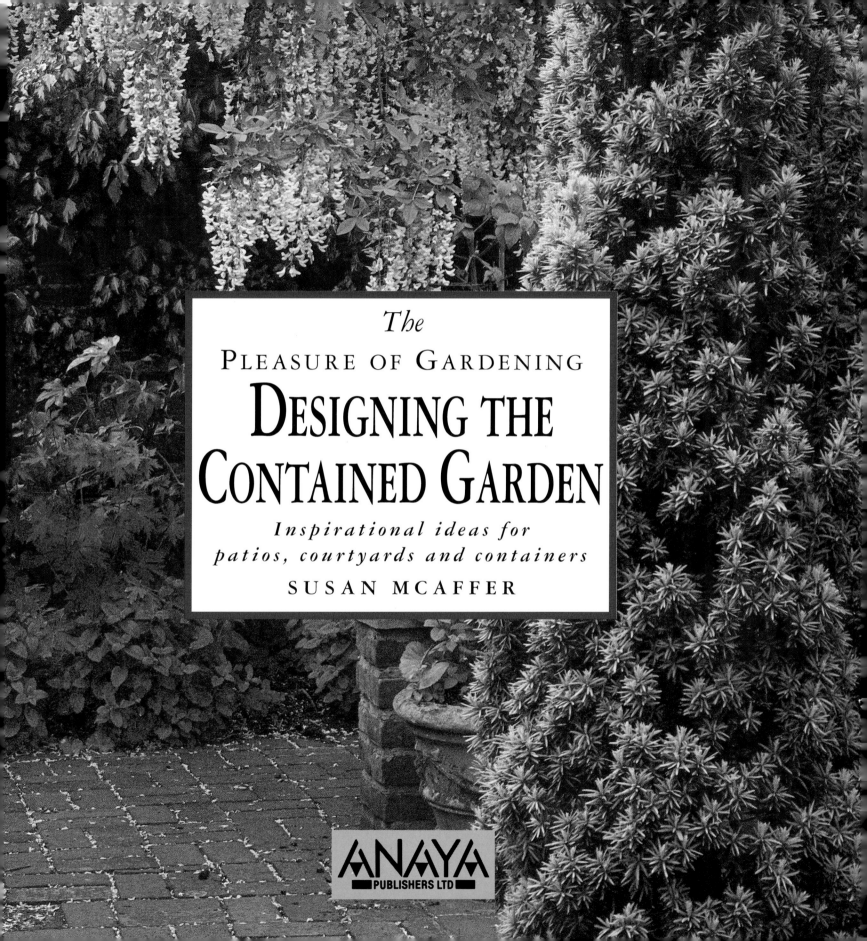

The
PLEASURE OF GARDENING
DESIGNING THE
CONTAINED GARDEN

*Inspirational ideas for
patios, courtyards and containers*

SUSAN MCAFFER

ANAYA
PUBLISHERS LTD

CONTENTS

Introduction

When I was a child I frequently spent my holidays with my grandparents, who owned a modest suburban house set in a quite remarkable garden. Originally a flat rectangle of space, that area had been transformed into a haven of plants, trees and secret corners nestled away from the busy road passing the front door. As the seasons changed, trees took their turn to flower, shrubs and perennials filled the borders and softened edges and, no matter how bleak or how hot the weather, that small garden always had something of interest to offer.

My early appreciation of the happy times I spent playing in that garden turned to admiration in later years when I first attempted to develop—with little enduring success—my own small enclosed garden at the back of a town house I was living in. I thought back to

LEFT: In this small city courtyard or patio immediate impact has been introduced with a selection of colourful flowering plants to brighten the area. Pots of zonal and ivy-leafed geraniums (Pelargonium), fuchsia, roses, lilies (Lilium), petunias and pansies are in full bloom and can easily be replaced as the season lengthens and new varieties become more appropriate. What could otherwise have been a dull area has become a charming space to enjoy. Designed by Ann Alexander-Sinclair.

my grandparents' property, and realised that without the right creative concept, detailed layout and complementary planting scheme, there was little hope of achieving anything like their much-admired space. So, with pencil and paper, I spent many hours working on my design and planning what I wanted to achieve before I wasted effort on digging and money on plants. The results were not perfect, but over the years, as my knowledge grew and our family moved from house to house, I became more confident about designing and developing gardens.

Today, with the pressures of an ever-growing population, our homes have become increasingly important to us. Designing and decorating the interior of our homes to provide a background to our lifestyle has become a popular occupation. To extend our living and working environment, we can, with imagination, also make the most of any outside area that is available to us. The creation of a patio or courtyard garden, decorated to complement our internal living rooms, can successfully transform an often unused backyard into another enjoyable space for all the family to use.

The terms 'patio' or 'courtyard garden' are used to describe either an area directly adjacent to the house or an intimate enclosure situated within a larger garden.

This style of garden offers a number of advantages. For example, it provides a framework within which any type of garden layout and style can be developed. It also offers privacy, and creates a micro-climate in which a wide range of plants can be successfully cultivated. An illusion of walls can be created with plants, or constructed from trellis panels, or made with permanent building materials.

The tradition of courtyard gardening has been with us for centuries. The need to protect animals, crops and homes from intruders first forced people to construct boundary walls around cultivated areas. Later generations, in various lands, turned this necessity into a virtue. They used the enclosures they created to provide shelter and warmth, and the fabric of the walls to support a wide range of plants.

Gardening, like any other skill, takes time to learn, but the enjoyment and pleasure that can be gained from this occupation are immeasurable.

In the first chapter of this book is a series of charming and workable garden designs and planting schemes which can be used in a variety of garden situations. The emphasis is on designing a total space in much the same way as you would design a total room.

The second chapter includes plants suitable for smaller gardens. Particular

emphasis has been placed on selections that will provide the best displays in an intimate garden area where everything is on show all the year around. Decorative details, such as seating, arbours, pergolas and topiary, are often included in a patio or courtyard, and some suggestions on styles and how to select items follow in the third chapter. The first section of the book concludes, in chapter four, with practical notes on maintaining the area you have created.

In the second section the emphasis changes to the use of containers, which is a fascinating gardening art, and one that is growing in popularity as more people live in apartments and town houses where space is at a premium. The plan included in chapter five for a complete container garden provides suggestions for those who may want to move plants around, or perhaps shift their garden to a different location at a future date.

A mixed planting scheme in containers is an art form, and some suggestions for different colour themes are also included which will help you to think about developing a mini-garden in this way.

Like the other lists of plants in this book, those for containers in chapter

LEFT: A clever layout has turned this small courtyard or patio garden at the rear of a city house into an enjoyable living space. The dense perimeter planting which includes variegated ivy, climbing roses and Clematis, *screens the area and provides a sound barrier from neighbours. The choice of a gentle grey paving for the total area with white furnishings helps to lighten the space. Designed by Helen Preston.*

six have been selected on the basis of their suitability and to provide 'choice' species for the best display. And finally, chapter seven details the practical side of container maintenance.

I have been fortunate in being able to travel around the world and have learned about gardening styles and design by visiting many famous gardens. There are numerous gardens, open to the public, which have provided me with inspiration. Most have their own unique style, and they invariably emphasise design as well as planting. In England, Hidcote Manor, Sissinghurst Castle, Nymans, Tintinhull and Knightshayes Court, to name just a few, are models from which much can be learned about developing a total concept, and within that concept establishing intimate, enclosed garden spaces.

In Europe the tradition of gardening goes back to the earliest times, and there are many private and public gardens that are very special, including the Italian Renaissance villas of La Gamberaia outside Florence, Villa Marcello near Padua, Villandry in Touraine, France, and the Garden of Hearts adjoining the Van Buuren Museum in Brussels.

In the United States different styles of enclosed gardens have evolved over the years. The Cloisters in New York is a fine example of a monastery courtyard garden

RIGHT: At the Chateau de Villandry, France, the true art of kitchen gardening can be seen at its most glorious. Laid out as a formal parterre, with its garden beds edged with box or decorative trellis, the walled garden or potager boasts a magnificent combination of vegetables, herbs and flowers.

which has recently been replanted in its original style. And the gardens of Filoli near San Francisco include a formal structure of walls and hedges where annuals bloom in a variety of colours.

One of the most beautiful examples of a courtyard garden developed in the United States in recent times is the work of the eminent English garden designer Russell Page who, in 1972, was asked for a temporary design for a bare plot of land at one end of a New York East Side art museum known as the Frick Collection. Amidst the rush and bustle of this cosmopolitan city, Page created a courtyard garden of immense charm and simplicity. Yet he had to deal with a range of design problems which many of us face when we consider our own plot of land: the space he had to work with was limited in size, it was overshadowed by tall buildings, thus giving little sun, and a solution was required that would look good throughout the seasons.

Page's design demonstrates clearly what can be achieved when all the practical layout tools are put into practice. He established a courtyard garden which has one clear creative concept. He achieved an harmonious relationship between the scale of the garden and its surrounding walls. He added texture in the form of interesting but simple planting combinations to enhance the garden's structure. And finally, he directly related the materials used for the seating and paths and the surrounds of a small central pool to the colour and materials of the museum. The courtyard garden of the Frick Collection has now become a permanent and much admired feature in New York City.

GARDENS IN EARLY TIMES

In Egypt the earliest recorded gardens were developed around 3000 BC. These gardens were formal, and established the tradition of separate compartments divided by walls and arbours. Containers were used along a path or wall to highlight the symmetry of the design. Long periods of relative stability and peace afforded the early Egyptians the opportunity of studying the arts and horticulture.

Because of the hot climate, irrigation was always a challenge. The commonly used formal square or rectangular layout of the gardens of the Egyptians was dictated by the need for a regular water supply for the plants. Fortunately for the wealthy owners of these lush enclosures, there was a ready and abundant supply of slave labour to raise water from the River Nile. The development of the early water canals from this period has been a major factor in garden design for other cultures throughout history.

The paradise gardens of Persia were the creations of an autocratic king and his court, and are recorded in writings and in elaborately woven carpet rugs and hangings. They were enclosed, park-like gardens of magnificent proportions with their perimeter walls planted with grape vines, climbers and fruit trees. Cool clear pools were a prominent design feature of these gardens and were part of the recreation areas located near the living quarters.

The influence of the Moorish gardens spread throughout north Africa and into parts of Italy and southern Spain. The style consisted of several decorative and intimate enclosed gardens surrounded by buildings and high walls which provided shelter and privacy. Fountains, water channels and pools were major features, and these devices were often used to link one area to another.

Good examples of these gardens, such as those at the Palace of the Alhambra and the Generalife in Granada, can still be found in areas of Spain, where the highly developed and stylised Moorish architecture is very distinctive.

The Spanish took this gardening style with them on their voyages of discovery around the world. Although the Spaniards who originally conquered areas of South America had little interest in gardening, and destroyed the beautiful gardens developed by the Aztecs, later settlers developed their own interpretation of the enclosed gardens they had known at home.

THE ANCIENT GREEKS
Although the Greeks were great philosophers and brought to the world a love of poetry and the arts, they developed very little in the way of domestic or pleasure gardening, concentrating mainly on food crops and vines.

The ancient Greeks did, however, leave two important legacies. They were the first to beautify public recreation areas by planting trees and shrubs in city squares and by adorning temples with flower pots. Secondly, they perfected a domestic style of architecture with a central columned courtyard or 'peristyle' incorporated into the building. Used as an outdoor living area, this was adorned with flowers in pots and often contained a small formal garden.

In Constantinople, for example, which was founded in the fourth century AD, many of the houses built for the wealthy commonly had peristyle gardens. This style of architecture also spread to many other areas of Europe and has survived in certain forms in both public and private dwellings to the present day.

THE ROMAN INFLUENCE

The Romans dictated fashion and style in Europe for about five hundred years. They created splendid gardens and the formal styles they favoured spread throughout western Europe. Their nature and extent can be visualised from Roman writings and from actual garden sites, particularly good examples of which are to be found in the towns of Pompeii near Naples, and Herculaneum south of Rome.

Wealthy Romans built luxury villas and country houses; the middle class lived in town houses with a small enclosed garden which, for much of the year, served as a room in the open air. However, many Romans, much like their counterparts today, lived in small apartments. These often featured a window box, which Pliny (*c.* 23/24–79 AD), the distinguished Roman philosopher and writer, described in this way: 'The common people of Rome offered the eye a reflection of the country with their miniature gardens in their windows.'

RIGHT: In New York, The Cloisters provides a particularly interesting example of a medieval courtyard garden in a style which generally evolved during the latter stages of the Dark Ages. One important aspect of this type of garden was to grow herbs for medicinal as well as culinary purposes.

THE DARK AGES

With the demise of the Roman Empire, the emphasis on living for pleasure, let alone gardening for pleasure, was forsaken in the face of a developing religious fervour culminating in the Dark Ages. In the monasteries and convents of the time, gardens were strictly utilitarian, producing vegetables, herbs for healing, and fruit from an occasional tree.

Later, more pleasingly aesthetic developments took place, with gardens containing combinations of herbs, flowers and vegetables; and in the great castles and palaces that dotted the landscape, enclosed gardens slowly began to appear, with a bed or two of herbs planted for medicinal or culinary purposes. For the middle and lower classes, however, life was taken up with hard manual work and the only gardening undertaken was the production of a few food crops.

In the twelfth century, secular gardens improved. However, it is not until the early sixteenth century that any advance in the development of garden style is clearly recorded. By this time, much horticultural knowledge and many treasure-troves of ancient relics that had been used to adorn buildings and gardens had been lost in the turbulent passage of the centuries. Nevertheless, some of the basic design and planting principles survived or were recreated and the development of many of the garden styles we know today dates back to this period.

EUROPE AND THE NEW WORLD

ENGLISH GARDENS

The English, who were not as frequently confined to walled towns as their European neighbours, developed larger gardens. These were often walled or hedged and divided into separate areas or rooms. They featured formal, raised flower beds, perhaps with a turf border, and fountains and springs were popular, as were decorative features, such as arbours, pergolas, topiaries, labyrinths and mazes.

Potted flowers and fruit trees also became popular, as did the now-famous 'knot' gardens which featured plants set in small geometric garden beds, often edged with clipped dwarf shrubs or a herb. Elaborate shapes, such as the arabesque or the ribbon pattern, were sometimes filled with coloured soil or gravel.

During the reign of Queen Elizabeth I — sometimes referred to as the Virgin Queen and often shown in portraits as Flora, the godess of flowers — English navigators and explorers brought back from the New World a wealth of new plant materials including exotic sub-tropical and tropical species which were eagerly seized upon and trialed in many gardens. However, despite this, landscape designs from Italy and France continued to dominate the English scene.

RIGHT: Developed around the ancient towers of Sissinghurst Castle, the gardens of Sissinghurst are laid out in a series of walled garden rooms each interlinked by paths and doorways. Colour plays a major role in each of the planting schemes, with borders composed in claret, blue, white and silver. Excellent use of vistas and focal points adds to the charm of this exceptional piece of garden design. In the foreground of this area a Magnolia x soulangeana *stands out against a background of* Clematis montana.

THE LANDSCAPE MOVEMENT

By the early eighteenth century, however, commentators like Joseph Addison and Alexander Pope favoured a natural landscape style, rather than the formality of French and Italian garden design. Addison wrote frequent essays about the subject in *The Spectator* and *The Tatler*. These ideas were later expounded by Stephen Switzer in 1718 in his three-volume publication *Ichnographica Rustica*.

The first major changes to a significant property appear to have been made by Thomas Bridgeman, who helped to replan the royal gardens at Richmond and Kensington. William Kent also followed this new landscape style, earning the title 'the father of modern gardening'. His ideas were later taken up and extended by Lancelot (Capability) Brown, who changed the face of English gardening forever from formal stylised arrangements to open plans where the objective was to suggest that all the surrounding countryside was part of a particular estate.

In England and elsewhere there was much spirited debate about this dramatic change to gardening style because, to achieve the landscaped look, many garden features in the vicinity of a house were demolished. The grand avenues, walls and hedges, box-lined paths, mazes, ponds, fountains, and statues all disappeared.

Humphrey Repton, a landscape gardener who took up this career after losing his family income, first followed Brown's ideas, but later refined the concept and went back to a more formal space near the home with detailing and beds of flowers. As time progressed, he went on to develop a large number of gardens fol-lowing a scheme he first proposed for Woburn. On that occasion he arranged a series of garden rooms, including a terrace and a parterre near the house, and a private garden for family use. This was a radical departure from Brown's ideal landscape.

The English idea of garden design was reproduced throughout areas of Europe. The French sensibly saved the formal gardens they had created and simply added a pastoral scene to them.

While the wealthy developed their parks and formal rooms, the middle and working classes were becoming more interested in pleasure gardening and could gain access to new gardening information through books and magazines. Notable works were those by the Scotsman John Claudius Loudon and his wife, Jane.

Loudon published a prolific number of books and articles during his lifetime and his wife carried on this work after his death in 1843. Her publications, *The Ladies' Flower Garden* and *The Ladies' Companion to the Flower Garden*, provided evidence that women's skills in the garden were finally coming to the fore in what had previously been a field dominated by men.

VICTORIAN ENGLAND

In the Victorian era, two names stand out—those of William Robinson and Gertrude Jekyll. Both published material and personally designed and supervised the planting of many gardens. The basis of the English style, as we know it today, is generally attributed to them.

Victorian gardens, often incorporating flowers such as pelargonium, calceolaria, verbena, petunia, delphinium and lark-spur, were, in the main, formal with a geometric layout. Robinson espoused the natural garden. Jekyll followed his lead with her personal versions which emphasised colour, shape and texture. Their work coincided with a growing interest in the restoration of smaller country houses and cottages.

Gertrude Jekyll also encouraged inner city dwellers to consider their backyards or forecourts. However, it was generally felt that the pollution of the times would allow few plants to develop and grow outside the house. Poorer families, with little money to spare for luxuries, were more likely to invest in a potted palm to adorn the front parlour than to attempt an outside garden.

THE ITALIAN RENAISSANCE

The Italian Renaissance started around the early fifteenth century. Initially, the gardens followed traditional formal layouts and were contained within enclosing walls. Later, with the advent of palatial villas, a new style of gardening layout developed, both within the cities and in the surrounding countryside.

Gardens were planted so that they gradually led the visitor up a series of terraces to a plateau where the villa was located. Here, the best outlook was

RIGHT: A series of beautiful garden rooms surrounds the mellow stone walls of Hazelbury Manor in Wiltshire, England. Within the framework of clipped green hedges the flower beds are intersected with pathways, and the inclusion of some beautiful pieces of ancient sculpture and statuary highlights the geometric layout.

provided from an open courtyard. This new style imposed architectural order, symmetry, perspective and proportion on a garden site. It also created a pleasant retreat and established a relationship between the house, the gardens and the other buildings in one comprehensive plan.

Italy was blessed with a number of great artists and craftsmen, such as Michelangelo, Raphael, Castiglione and Peruzzi. Their talents were employed by the clergy and the wealthy to create some magnificent buildings. Cardinal Giuliano de Medici created the Villa Madama with, it is believed, the help of Raphael. This complex was designed as a suite of garden rooms rather than a house. Pirro Ligorio, a Neapolitan painter and architect, planned the beautiful gardens of the Villa d'Este. These were terraced down a hillside and featured a splendid walk of one hundred water stairs.

In Rome, the architect Bramante developed the plan for a magnificent papal garden, linking the Vatican Palace to the Villa Belvedere by a series of courtyards. The fame of this garden and others such as the Villa Farnese, upon which the gardens at Dorchester House in London were modelled, inspired creations in other areas of Italy and further afield.

LEFT: This exceptionally pretty enclosed garden was designed by Thomas Church, the noted American garden designer. His layout of a smartly clipped box (Buxus sempervirens), parterre and topiary is softened by the addition of pink roses and hydrangeas.

THE FRENCH STYLE

During the first half of the sixteenth century, France was embroiled in armed conflict with Spain. This period was followed by the religious wars, so there was little time for the development of gardens until the seventeenth century when more peaceful times permitted the owners of the moated chateaux to move their formal gardens outside the boundary walls.

Many gardens, like the semicircular one surrounding half of the chateau Montargis, were used mainly for growing vegetables and fruit. However, alongside these, small rectangular and circular parterres or formally patterned and edged gardens were beginning to be developed.

These striking features were also used in the plans of other gardens, such as those belonging to the chateaux of Fontainebleau, Blois, Gaillon and Valeri. Indeed, the scope was almost limitless because, as Bernard Palissy, the author of a treatise on waterworks and fountains, noted, 'There are more than four thousand noble houses in France.'

Gardening literature had become popular reading by the mid-sixteenth century. One early manuscript was *La Maison Rustique*, originally published in Latin as *Praedium Rusticum* in 1554, and translated into English in 1600.

The 'grand opera' of French garden design came when Le Nôtre—following in the tradition of Etienne Dupeyrac and Claude Mollet—created the gardens of Versailles. This magnificent estate, designed to cater to the taste of the court of Louis XIV, is a vast outdoor drawing room, featuring fountains, alleys, garden statuary, enclosures and buildings.

The stylised layouts and features of these gardens were later used as the basis for planning gardens around other chateaux and, later still, around more humble manor houses. Grand and elegant, these gardens were more for show than for quiet family enjoyment. To cater for the latter, it was usual to find within the layout, and associated with the living quarters, a secret enclosed garden for family use. This was an idea also used in many of the grand gardens in Italy.

THE NEW WORLD

In the New World, settlers took with them their knowledge and ideas of traditional garden styles. After a slow start, Americans took up gardening with enthusiasm and a lively trade in seeds and plants developed between the Old and the New Worlds. Settlers had to learn how to cope with conditions ranging from freezing to sub-tropical to desert.

Many magnificent private and public gardens were developed over the years, and a host of landscape specialists from many regions made significant contributions. Two notable designers were Loutrell Briggs and Thomas Church. Briggs settled in South Carolina, in the 1930s and specialised in designing small walled city gardens based on concepts from the eighteenth and nineteenth centuries. Church lived and worked in San Francisco, designing more than two thousand gardens and was well established by the 1950s.

Around the world today, there is wide variety of gardening styles incorporating the principles of past work. Many are open to the public and are an eclectic mixture of both formal and informal layouts.

COURTYARD & PATIO DESIGNS

The Entrance Garden

All gardens are individual. They offer scope for the most elaborate designs or for a simple formal layout. The small scale of contemporary gardens makes careful attention to detail extremely important.

The idea of an entrance garden is to provide a welcome. However, often it is dull and uninspiring, limited in size and overshadowed by trees or other buildings. As a result, it is regarded as a space to pass through and not to linger in or enjoy. But like any other garden area around the home its limitations can be overcome with careful planning and detailing, imagination and flair.

An entrance should establish a style and provide a glimpse of what is in store for the visitor. Begin planning the space by viewing it from all angles—from the garden, from the road, from the house and from any windows that overlook the area. Charting what exists from a bird's eye view will reveal existing form.

The overall design must be precisely thought out and the main axes and vistas established first. Make access to the main door clear, so that any visitor is directed towards it immediately. When creating paths or walls use building materials that relate, in scale and finish, to the house. Adopt one simple strong creative idea as more than one will almost certainly create chaos. The concept must also provide the answer to such utilitarian problems as what to do with the family car and how to provide adequate security. Finally, as this area is always on show, it is important to limit the amount of work needed to maintain the appearance of the garden.

Choosing the plant material for a small enclosed garden is more difficult than for larger open areas. Because all the space is usually on show throughout the year, plants must look attractive in the different seasons. Studying plants in the immediate neighbourhood will reveal what grows well. Choosing material that offers good texture and form is the basis of any successful planting scheme.

Special features, such as a seasonal show of bulbs, can be introduced by planting them in containers. They can then be removed and replaced when flowering is over. Alternatively add a piece of sculpture or topiary.

LEFT: The tiny below ground level entrance garden of this inner-city apartment has been greatly enhanced by the careful use of colours and planting. The terracotta pavers provide a warm background colour to the area and the predominantly green planting scheme will look attractive throughout the year with little maintenance. The strong architectural shape of the Fatsia japonica *with its glossy green leaves contrasts nicely with the touch of colour which appears in the selection of annuals planted in the window-box and the hybrid* Clematis *growing on the trellis. Designed by Keyes Landscape.*

PREVIOUS PAGE: A beautifully orchestrated walled garden has been designed to suit a country home. Full advantage has been made of surrounding trees and the green palette has been accentuated by the limited introduction of colour to the garden area. Planting has been contained by neatly hedged garden beds and the dramatic arches in the brick walls have been underscored with the addition of foliage trained to emphasise the shape of the arch. Designed by Ann Griot.

Plan for a small entrance garden

This beautifully structured entrance garden, which will look good from both the
street and from inside the house, will greatly add to the visual appeal of any home. The
simple planting scheme will work well in a range of locations including areas overshadowed
by buildings or trees, and the plants themselves will reach maturity quickly if they
are well fed, watered and clipped regularly.

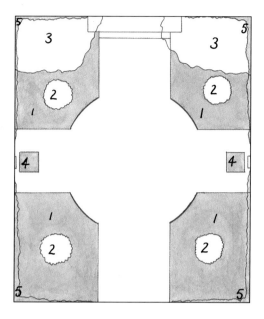

Key to planting scheme

1 *Buxus sempervirens*
2 *Ilex aquifolium*
3 *Crataegus x lavallei* 'Carrierei' (standard)
4 Annuals
5 *Hedera helix* (to cover walls)

This elegant entrance courtyard or patio sets the scene for an inner city townhouse. Its strong formal structure creates an immediate sense of arrival and offers visitors and residents a chance to pause and enjoy this garden room with its simple beauty.

The garden has been created out of a tiny scrap of land. Overhanging trees and surrounding buildings limit the amount of natural sunlight that can be expected in areas like this and severely restrict the range of plants that can be successfully grown. In this instance, the design provides a green framework to set off the two Regency urns on either side of the central path. In these urns seasonal plantings will create an eye-catching focal point within the garden.

Essentially, the garden has been divided into four planting areas. Each is planted with massed box (*Buxus sempervirens*) clipped to a height of 40cm (15in), which creates a panel of solid green. A clipped holly (*Ilex aquifolium*) topiary is centred in each bed. Framing the doorway to the house are two standard hawthorns (*Crataegus x lavallei* 'Carrierei'). This French hybrid forms a small tree which has clusters of white flowers followed by pear-shaped orange-red fruit.

The severe dark format creates an interesting area to look at through all the seasons, and is particularly appealing viewed from the upstairs windows of the house as well as from the road. The paving is granite sets, which are the ideal shape to form both the round central space and the paths. Lighting is important in an entrance garden. Here underlighters for the urns provide a subtle wash of illumination within the framework.

To create this garden design successfully, it is essential to get the form right first and to complete all the structural requirements at the outset. The walls should be as uniform as possible. Some people are lucky enough to have beautiful brick walls, and these can be lightly covered with ivy (*Hedera helix*). Where a range of finishes has to be contended with, the best solution might be to plaster the surrounding walls before planting.

Plants in this garden, if well fed, watered and clipped regularly, can easily reach maturity in a few years, and will provide a classic, easily maintained entrance garden.

The formal walled garden

The formal walled garden is perhaps one of the most influential garden styles. With its symmetrical layout, edges of garden beds lined with clipped box, centres abundantly planted, and walls of brick or hedge clothed in flowering climbers, it epitomises most people's perception of the typical English garden.

In a formal walled garden, trellis work can be used to create the illusion of walls if you do not have the patience to wait for a yew or a Leyland cypress or a laurel hedge to grow, or if you are not fortunate enough to have structural walls available.

Privacy, colour and peace are the hallmarks of the walled garden. Its familiar style can be created by using a large number of different plants, or masses of one kind of plant, within a formal framework.

One such garden is Hidcote Manor, set in the windswept hills of the English Cotswolds. It was designed by the

LEFT: The soft greys, lavenders and pinks of Ageratum, Salvia and Cleome create a romantic mood for the summer planting of the flower beds within the formal walled garden at Wisley in Surrey, England. In direct contrast, and to maintain a formal note, dark green clipped box and yew topiary mark the start of pathways and stand out against the lush rambling climbers which have been used to clothe the brick walls. A frame of trellis has been attached to the bricks to take the weight of the wall planting, and will look good during periods of less rampant growth.

French-born American, Major Lawrence Johnston, and is regarded by many as the best example of this truly English style, with its formal planning and informal planting.

Johnston created a series of garden rooms in 1905 out of a bare site. By the time he had finished, the area was terraced and a series of geometrically designed gardens was completed, each with its own special feature such as a pergola, pool or gazebo. The walls of the rooms were created by planting hedges of yew, box, holly and hornbeam and by mingling hornbeam, yew, beech and holly together in a tapestry hedge. The principal section of the garden near the house is the courtyard. Here, hydrangeas, hypericum, *Magnolia delavayi*, hoherias, and the climber *Solanum crispum* grow amongst other plants, creating a beautiful effect.

Gertrude Jekyll left behind a rich heritage of gardening knowledge and experience. It is perhaps her work with mixed herbaceous borders that is regarded by many as the best example of the formal English style of gardening. Sadly, however, there are few actual examples of her planting schemes left today. One exception is Hestercombe in Somerset.

Jekyll and the architect Sir Edwin Lutyens worked on many projects including Hestercombe. The basic layout for this project divided the gardens into a series of walled rooms. Near the house

they are small and formal, but further away the style becomes more relaxed.

In her time, Gertrude Jekyll wrote prolifically on gardening and was generous in her descriptions of planting schemes and colour combinations. She encouraged gardeners setting out to plant a bed or border, to aim for a luxuriant feel by softening lines and hard edges. To create a soft effect, she also used material in clumps, with several examples of each plant dovetailed together.

Lutyens also worked on another great garden when he was employed to assist with the restoration of the house and the garden outline at Great Dixter on the Kent and Sussex border. This garden was started in 1910 on a site which, until that time, had been a farmyard containing a range of red brick farm buildings.

The garden is split into a series of enclosed garden rooms including a sunken garden, a rose garden and a courtyard garden. The owner at the time, Nathaniel Lloyd, was an architectural historian and topiary enthusiast. Examples of his topiary skills are used to great effect throughout the garden and especially in an area known as the topiary lawn.

The herbaceous borders set in the Walled Garden at Nymans were designed by William Robinson. They are backed with trees and shrubs while the foreground is set with thousands of spring-flowering bulbs.

Plan for a formal walled garden

Following the best traditions of the famous English walled gardens, this design aims
to provide an area of charm and beauty throughout the year. A palette of creams, apricot
and buff has been used within a formal framework.

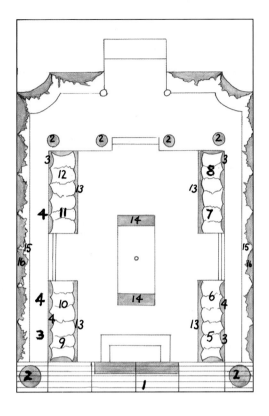

Key to planting scheme

1 *Wisteria venusta*
2 *Buxus sempervirens*
3 *R.* 'Penelope'
4 *R.* 'Prosperity'
5 *R.* 'Chanelle'
6 *R.* 'Nancy Steen'
7 *R.* 'French Lace'
8 *R.* 'Margaret Merril'
9 *R.* 'Cream Delight'
10 *R.* 'Grüss an Aachen'
11 *R.* 'Julia's Rose'
12 *R.* 'Apricot Nectar'
13 *Aurinia saxatilis*
14 *Iris ensata*
15 *Nepeta x faassenii*
16 Climbing roses:
    R. 'Alchemist'
    R. 'Alister Stella Gray'
    R. 'Buff Beauty'
    R. 'Céline Forestier'
    R. 'Cloth of Gold'
    R. 'Desprez à Fleurs Jaunes'
    R. 'Gloire de Dijon'
    R. 'Graham Thomas'
    R. 'Maréchal Niel'

To set the scene for this formal brick-walled courtyard or patio, a shaded pergola covered with *Wisteria venusta* forms the entrance into a simple lobby decorated with a frame of trellis. Stepping out of the lobby you find yourself on a gravel path, two steps above the sunken garden area.

Form is everything, and although the planting is a beautiful mix of apricot, buff and cream roses, it is the detail of the layout which makes it a truly charming garden. An Edwardian shingled summerhouse overlooks the lawn and sunken pool with planting of Japanese irises at either end. The brick walls have panels of trellis attached to them so that even when the roses are bare there is attractive trellage as decoration. Whitewashed terracotta pots are planted with standard box trees (*Buxus sempervirens*) to add to the formal Edwardian look. They can be moved into the summerhouse in the frosty weather to avoid any damage.

Old-fashioned roses with lovely subtle colours grow on the walls. Many are recurrent, with extended flowering seasons, and a number are notable for their fine fragrance. In the garden beds, which you initially look down on from the paths—thereby gaining the very best view of the leaves and flowers—are the modern floribundas, which will produce clusters of roses rather than long stiff branches. Finally, the hybrid musk roses, 'Prosperity' and 'Penelope', tumble over the low brick walls, breaking the line of the path.

This garden, with its mix of French lace colours in the roses, its formal terracotta brick walls, its lawn and its water feature, is unashamedly beautiful. This is a very memorable area.

The inner city garden

The typical city garden has undergone a metamorphosis in recent years. As inner city areas have been redeveloped into working and living environments, the old backyard of the 1930s, with its polluted atmosphere, has gradually disappeared.

Interestingly, it was the Dutch who were among the first in Europe to make the most of their small backyards. In the sixteenth century land was scarce making it difficult for many to own large properties. Indeed, it was the norm for even the wealthy to have only a small open area behind a town house.

The conventional layout for these retreats was neat and simple. A wall around each side created a square or rectangular area, which was generally laid out with four paths meeting at a fountain in the centre. Flower beds were outlined with a low hedge of box, and flowers were arranged in neat rows with one species to each bed.

By the seventeenth century more ornaments and details were preferred, and balustrades, urns and statues were incorporated. Because the moralists of the time frowned on the growing trend for flowers, the garden was likely to contain only a modest planting of fruit trees trained against the walls and a laburnum or an elder grown for its ornamental foliage and fruit. This type of planting scheme was swept away in later years by the Dutch craze for growing tulips in all shapes and colours.

The Japanese influence on gardens is interesting. They cultivated few flowers as their main interest in creating small private courtyards was in their form and in the relationship of a few specifically placed items. Early Japanese gardens were a place for contemplation, and their design was influenced by Zen Buddhism. The Zen masters taught the Japanese to create an area of tranquillity using dry landscapes of gravel, sand and rocks chosen for shape, colour, and growth of lichens. A cherry or plum tree was favoured as much for its blossom as its fruit.

Like their European counterparts, the Japanese live in densely populated areas and the ability to create a beautiful space out of a few square yards of ground has always been a high priority.

Adaptations of the Japanese style of garden are sometimes seen in other countries. The end result can be spectacularly successful if the project is well planned and, in particular, if it relates to the architectural style of the building. This style became particularly popular on the west coast of America.

LEFT: This inner city enclosed garden, with its lush planting and simple but imaginative layout, is an excellent example of what can be achieved in a limited space. Areas for all the members of the family to enjoy have been included, and a feeling of additional space has been achieved by changes of level and green barriers. The total design is beautifully harmonised by using a simple clay paver and furnishings which suit the style of garden and add to its architectural detailing. Designed by Michael Balston.

Plan for an inner city garden

A typical inner city garden, which includes a side yard and small courtyard or patio.
The technique of false perspective has been used to create an interesting area out of the
narrow side passage. The addition of an harmonious planting scheme combined with a small
water feature, creates a very livable area which will be particularly appealing at night.

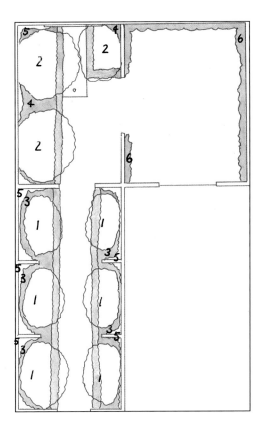

Key to planting scheme

1 *Laburnum x watereri* (standard)
2 *Gleditsia triacanthos*
3 *Viburnum davidii*
4 *Aucuba japonica*
5 *Hedera helix*
6 *Hydrangea anomala petiolaris*

This garden mirrors all the problems people find themselves faced with when designing gardens in cities today. However, with the right approach and by using techniques of false perspective, this type of space can become—particularly at night—an oasis away from the surrounding bustle of the city.

Sometimes, when approaching a design problem, it is the disadvantages of the site that need to be built upon. In this instance, the drama of a dark space has been increased with the addition of more trees to overshadow the area. At night they create a sense of theatre, which ensures that the eye is focused into the garden and away from the dreariness of neighbouring walls and windows. Lighting and the sound of tinkling water add to the atmosphere.

When the space is viewed from the window of the house, the narrowness of the long corridor of garden is emphasised by the tapering of the brick path towards the water feature. This small dark pool, which will reflect just a glimmer of light at night, is backed by a mirror enclosed with a trellis surround.

The planting is green and tranquil making a low-maintenance space which can be enjoyed all year around. Ivy (*Hedera helix*) is trained to smother the walls, and hedges of box (*Buxus sempervirens*) neatly enclose the underplanting of massed *Aucuba japonica* and *Viburnum davidii*. The six *Laburnum x watereri*, with their glossy leaves and long slender racemes, are contained within individual walled planting bays.

In the sunnier alcove near the house, a table and chairs are placed so that meals can be eaten out of doors in the warmer months. *Hydrangea anomala petiolaris* cloaks the surrounding walls, and in the summer and autumn its attractive large clusters of greenish-white flowers decorate the area.

The low-maintenance garden

Designing a low-maintenance garden to suit the lifestyle of busy people can be both fun and rewarding. This area can be as aesthetically pleasing as any other garden space, as long as the fundamental rules for achieving a balanced layout with an eye to form and scale are followed.

The major rule to bear in mind is that the whole area must be planned and developed at the same time. Start by assessing the needs of your family and how individual members will use the garden; also consider what will complement your house through all the seasons of the year.

There are basically two main ways to establish a low-maintenance courtyard or patio. The first is to create a formalised space with a lot of hard surface areas and a minimum of planting. The second is to create a wild garden with a mass of planting. Either solution will require some maintenance, as it is impossible in any outside environment to avoid this completely.

The first option has some advantages for the city dweller wanting to gain the maximum outside space for entertaining and relaxation. By using paving material that is the same as either the fabric of the house or the floor of the room leading out to the courtyard or patio, it is possible to extend the living spaces of the home visually and add a feeling of overall spaciousness to the property. Planting should ideally be restricted to raised beds for ease of maintenance, and seasonal effects can be added by using movable containers.

Additional features, such as a small pool, birdbath or special sculpture, can provide a focal point which will help to direct the eye into the garden and away from any ugly buildings surrounding it. Pergolas can provide both additional privacy and welcome shade near the house.

If the climate is mild enough to make outside dining at night a pleasure, special lighting and containers of plants that will scent the air after dark are worthwhile additions. Tobacco plants, particularly *Nicotiana alata* and *Nicotiana sylvestris*, and lilies, including the early flowering Madonna (*L.candidum*), followed by *L.regale* and finally the late summer/early autumn flowering *L. speciosum*, are all worth growing.

The initial financial outlay for paving and structural work can be a burden with this type of garden. However, if you intend to occupy the property for a long period, this will not be a major concern.

The second way to achieve a low-maintenance garden and one that provides an entirely different result is to plant a mass of ground-cover plants. In the wild, nature provides some excellent examples of how this works. Blackberry covering a bank or heather clothing a moorland grow with great vigour and produce such complete shade or root dominance that no other plants or weeds can exist. Ground-cover plants can be used in the same way to suppress weeds.

An added advantage of this style of planting comes from the natural economy that develops. The leaf cover shades the ground, preventing excess drying by the sun; the roots of the plants help to prevent soil-scouring in heavy rains; and the autumn and winter leaf fall provides a natural feeding mulch.

A full range of plants can be used for this type of planting. Shrubs and trees provide the backbone, but herbaceous plants, creepers, carpeting plants and even some ferns can be used successfully.

LEFT: This approach to a low-maintenance garden provides a comfortable area suitable for entertaining. Seasonal colours can be added by including more containers of annuals and perennials to contrast with the green topiary used to create the basis of the scheme. The choice of paving detail adds to the formality and enhances the feeling of easy care with its neat grid pattern. Designed by Tim du Val.

Plan for a wild low-maintenance garden

A design for a garden full of mystery and surprise. The two woodland dells, heavily planted with trees and ground cover plants, provide a low-maintenance scheme that once established will provide an inviting and interesting area all year round.

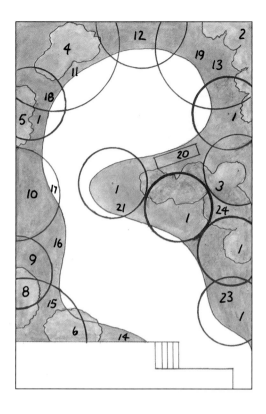

Key to planting scheme

1 *Betula pendula*
2 *Aucuba japonica*
3 *Rhododendron auriculatum*
4 *Hydrangea* 'White Wave'
5 *Spiraea* 'Arguta'
6 *Aesculus parviflora*
7 *Malus floribunda*
8 *Cotoneaster frigidus* 'Cornubia'
9 *Magnolia soulangeana* 'Lennei Alba'
10 *Prunus* 'Okame'
11 *Prunus serrulata* 'Shirotae'
12 *Amelanchier arborea*
13 *Ilex aquifolium*
14 *Liriope muscari*
15 *Hosta ventricosa*
16 *Epimedium grandiflorum*
17 *Vaccinium corymbosum*
18 *Pachysandra terminalis*
19 *Hypericum calycinum*
20 *Geranium endressii*
21 *Bergenia cordifolia*
22 *Cotoneaster dammeri*
23 *Skimmia japonica*
24 Bulbs:
     Galanthus nivalis
     Anemone nemorosa
     Hyacinthoides hispanica

This design and planting scheme can provide secret corners and tranquil areas for all the members of the family to enjoy. It is essentially a woodland garden, where light filters through the trees on to a mixture of greens and produces dappled patterns on the lawn.

The planting scheme is simple with nothing too difficult to grow or maintain. The European white birch (*Betula pendula*) has been chosen to give height and form to the area. These graceful trees, with their distinguished silver-white trunks, have mid-green diamond-shaped leaves. They are a fast growing tree, but have shallow greedy roots so the underplanting of shrubs has been specifically selected to cope with this. Here we find *Aucuba japonica* with its variegated leaves and red berries, *Rhododendron auriculatum* which has richly scented large white flowers in huge trusses, *Hydrangea* 'White Wave', and *Spiraea* 'Arguta' with its graceful slender branches smothered with small clusters of pure white flowers in both spring and summer.

To complement the form of the birch trees and to add a rich distinction to the garden, a *Magnolia x soulangiana* 'Lennei Alba' with its beautiful globular ivory-white flowers is planted next to a *Prunus* 'Okame' which has carmine-rose flowers and leaves that are an attractive colour in autumn.

The ground cover consists of densely planted compatible plants, each of which will stake out its own place in this area of semi-shade. For the spring, the trees have been underplanted with bulbs, and the edges of the lawn are planted with daffodils to add their bright colour to the dense layers of green.

To give visual interest and to add a sense of mystery, the total area has been broken into two spaces with the lawn narrowing into a tunnel under the trees. Mounds of earth have been built up to around 1.5m (4–5ft) to give instant height and additional interest to the ground-cover planting.

The lawn area is left rough, particularly in the back dell. Where the climate is suitable, it could be seeded to become a true meadow lawn, adding extra colour in spring and summer. The ground-cover plants spill over the edges of the lawn and require only the occasional trim to keep them in good shape.

The cottage garden

An unpretentious mixture of old-fashioned flowers, with herbs, vegetables and fruit trees offering ornamental value, is the image of the cottage garden. Charming and abundant, with flowers growing in profusion and with rambler roses and climbers covering the house and walls of the garden, this is a style that appeals to many people.

Cottage gardens have been with us for centuries. Originally created because of economic necessity, they were the gardens of the rural poor who used the land around their homes to grow vegetables and herbs. Flowers were added when seeds or cuttings could be gathered from the wild or traded with neighbours.

When later generations of lower middle class sprawled into the suburbs and craftsmen and artisans took up gardening, they followed the cottage garden tradition.

Fashions changed toward the end of the nineteenth century when the arts and crafts movement was born. Gardens surrounding smaller country estates were divided into garden rooms. The cottage garden style suited these enclosures, and although it was contained within a more formal framework, it was readily adopted.

Vita Sackville-West's garden at Sissinghurst is in essence a cottage-style garden with its lush planting. Within this great garden, there is an area specifically called 'the cottage garden', where flowers and herbs are planted in profusion around a large central verdigris copper pot.

The writer and cottage gardening enthusiast, Margery Fish, who created a delightful garden at East Lambrook Manor just after the Second World War, suggested that flowers like clove-scented pinks, roses, primroses, southernwood, hollyhocks, mignonette and lavender were the classic cottage plants. Honeysuckle, daisies, daffodils and true geraniums were also favourites which she delighted in growing.

The courtyard or patio is an ideal environment for this type of planting. The walls offer shelter from persistent winds; sunny corners can be used to advantage to grow tender flowering annuals and perennials; fruit trees and currant bushes can be trained to cover wall space.

Pergolas and trellis work look comfortable in cottage gardens and are ideal supports for rambler roses and flowering climbers. Simplicity of design and planting that makes the garden look as though nature has taken a hand are the key elements for success.

LEFT: This charming cottage garden at Lower Hall, Worfield, England, makes use of a variety of climbing and shrub roses to intermingle with the abundant planting typical of this type of garden. Drifts of white lavender edge the brick paths, and a seat is incorporated to catch the sun and provide a quiet spot to read or contemplate the pretty scene. Courtyards or patios which are sheltered and enjoy lots of sun are ideal for this planting style.

Plan for a cottage garden

To provide year-round interest, this cottage-style courtyard or patio has been planned to ensure that there is always something flowering, fruiting, budding, or displaying an interesting leaf colour. The mix of plants will delight any true plantsman with its colour combinations and imaginative juxtapositions.

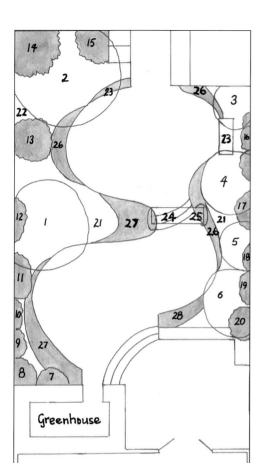

Key to planting scheme

1 *Prunus serrulata* 'Tai Haku'
2 *Cladrastris lutea*
3 *Sorbus* 'Joseph Rock'
4 *Magnolia denudata*
5 *Rhus typhina* 'Laciniata'
6 *Pyrus salicifolia* 'Pendula'
7 *Camellia saluenensis* 'Salutation' (espaliered)
8 *Chimonanthus praecox* (espaliered)
9 *Garrya elliptica* (espaliered)
10 *Escallonia* 'Donard seedling' (espaliered)
11 *Magnolia stellata* (espaliered)
12 *Hamamelis mollis* (espaliered)
13 *Viburnum plicatum* 'Lanarth'
14 *Viburnum rhytidophyllum*
15 *Ilex aquifolium*
16 *Hydrangea* 'White wave'
17 *Philadelphus x lemoinei* (espaliered)
18 *Philadelphus* 'Avalanche' (espaliered)
19 *Syringa persica* 'Alba' (espaliered)
20 *Olearia x scilloniensis*
21 *Rhododendron mucronatum* 'Album'
22 *Pachysandra terminalis*
23 *Arctostaphylos* 'Emerald Carpet'
24 *R.* 'Frühlingsgold'
25 *R.* 'Wedding Day'

26 Foliage for shady areas:
 Hosta
 Liriope muscari
 Bergenia cordifolia
 Helleborus
 Omphalodes cappadocica
 Pulmonaria angustifolia
 Polygonatum multiflorum
 Epimedium grandiflorum
 Cimicifuga racemosa
 Artemisia lactiflora
 Anemone x hybrida
 Acanthus spinosus

27 Blue theme:
 Delphinium
 Aster
 Aconitum nepellus
 Campanula persicifolia
 Geranium pratense
  'Buxton's Blue'
  'Johnson's Blue'

28 Grey theme:
 Lavandula angustifolia
 Achillea 'Moonshine'
 Alchemilla mollis
 Stachys byzantina
 Thalictrum delavayi

A successful cottage garden requires care, attention and enthusiasm. Success depends less on good lines than on achieving layers of interesting planting. It is a true plantsman's garden, where colour combinations and imaginative juxtapositions of plants can provide interest in every corner.

This design, which uses spring blossom, autumn berries, and masses of annuals and perennials for summer colour, offers the opportunity to create a pretty garden with year-round interest. The planting style is rich and abundant, rather like a controlled jungle. As a result, there is a high degree of maintenance required, with the job of pruning and shaping being of high priority to keep plants in scale.

Shrubs, selected to espalier against the walls, have also been specifically chosen to add additional colour or special interest. For example, the *Garrya elliptica* is a winter flowering shrub which produces magnificent grey-green catkins, and the *Escallonia* 'Donard Seedling' has abundant pink buds opening to white throughout summer and autumn.

The area is divided into two distinct sections creating a sense of space and mystery. Access to the second garden is up some shallow steps and through a pergola covered with the climbing roses 'Frühlingsgold' and 'Wedding Day'. 'Frühlingsgold' is a charming single rose of rich golden-yellow paling to primrose, and 'Wedding Day' is a vigorous climber which produces large trusses of single flowers with prominent yellow stamens. A seat is placed in this area to create a peaceful spot from which to contemplate the garden.

Planting in the brick-edged beds close to the home has a colour theme. Greys and blues form a gentle contrast against the massed planting of *Rhododendron mucronatum* 'Album', with its dull-green foliage and fragrant funnel-shaped flowers. Plants with distinctive foliage are suggested for the second garden area, which is shaded by the branched *Cladrastris lutea* in summer and lightened by its beautiful yellow foliage in autumn.

As maintenance is the key to providing on-going care, a shed with adequate storage room is necessary. Compost bins are a useful addition. A greenhouse also provides room to winter-over frost-tender pot plants and to propagate and start seedlings.

The kitchen and herb garden

Nothing can be more inspiring to the home cook than a beautifully laid out kitchen garden bursting with fresh produce ready to be picked for the next meal. As the seasons change the crops change, and the mix of vegetables and herbs, and salad plants and fruits enjoy their moment of full-grown sun-blushed glory.

All around the world, from the earliest times, kitchen gardens of one type or another have flourished. The Egyptians and the Romans were skilled at growing food crops and spread their knowledge throughout much of Europe.

In the Middle Ages, the study of herbal properties and their use in cooking and for medicinal purposes became the province of the clerics and monks.

Settlers in the New World took their horticultural knowledge with them, and food crops were quickly cultivated wherever settlements began. In America today, it is possible to see a reconstruction of the large kitchen garden George Washington developed at Mount Vernon in 1786 and Thomas Jefferson's garden at Monticello where he grew over 250 varieties of herbs and vegetables.

However, it is perhaps the French who developed the kitchen garden as an art form. With their love of cooking and extensive range of regional dishes, it is not surprising that they placed great store on growing crops well and on creating a visually attractive environment.

In the sixteenth century the French kitchen garden, known as the potager, was an essential part of grand gardens throughout the land. The potager were formally laid out, with neat regular patterns of gardening beds planted with vegetables and fruit. Walls were essential to protect the crops from wind and frost, and low hedges or edging were used around individual beds. Fruit trees were grown in pots. This was a skill perfected by the French and the Dutch, although the French first developed the art of growing fruit trees against walls. Later, particularly in England, it became fashionable to separate the various crops; and herbs in particular were planted in their own plots, often in knot gardens or in chequerboard patterns.

The popularity of growing fresh herbs waned in later times, and dried products became the norm on the kitchen shelf. Nowadays, this trend has been reversed, and small herb plots—known in America as door gardens—have again become a popular form of gardening.

LEFT: The potager garden at Bourton House in Gloucestershire, England, features a number of shaped garden beds containing different varieties of vegetables and herbs within a trim border of green variegated box. The warm stone walls provide an ideal environment for espaliered fruit trees or for currants and berries. This apple, Orleans Reinette, has been trained over the years to a good size and provides a fine crop of fruit during the season.

Plan for a kitchen and herb garden

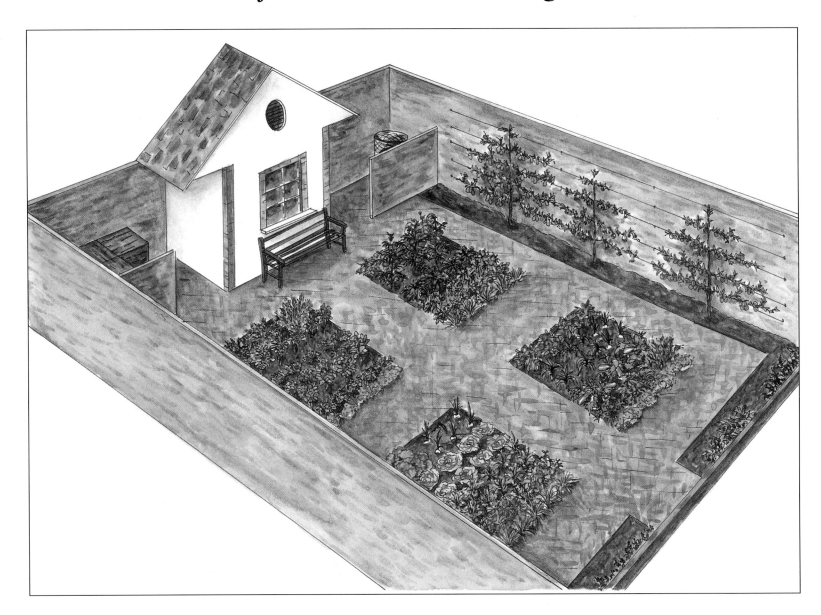

The layout of this kitchen garden is a simple one and will be enhanced by planting complementary and contrasting groups of colours and textures together. Herbs, fruit, vegetables and flowers can all be included to suit the household's requirements.

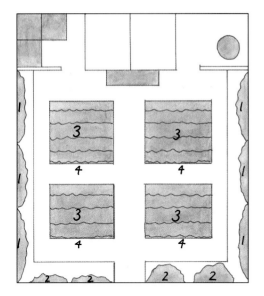

Key to planting scheme

1. Espaliered or fan-trained fruit trees
2 Currants or berries
3 Vegetables, herbs and flowers
4 Parsley or chives for edging
See page 44 for a selection of plants for a kitchen and herb garden.

To grow vegetables, herbs and fruit with success, a sheltered sunny site is necessary. A working area for composting and for storing implements and fertilisers is also needed as maintenance and replanting are continual.

The potting shed in this scheme is decorative and practical and has been designed to complement the style of the garden.

This courtyard or patio uses every inch of available space, with a simple layout of four bays allowing room for a mixture of planting schemes. The bays have been kept to a practical size for ease of maintenance. Fruit trees are planted down each side wall, and have been espaliered or fan-trained for easy harvesting, pruning and spraying. Bushes of gooseberries, currants, raspberries and blackberries can be grown at one sunny end of the garden. The result is a productive and ornamental planting scheme.

A list of vegetables and herbs suitable for a similar kitchen and herb garden is provided. The choice of plants will be determined by individual requirements. For visual appeal, try grouping the plants by height, foliage and family, and planting the garden edges with decorative herbs.

A SELECTION OF PLANTS FOR A KITCHEN AND HERB GARDEN

The planting list that follows includes a number of varieties of fruits, vegetables and herbs you may be interested in including in your own kitchen and herb garden. Check with your local plant nursery to see what varieties are available in your area and are best for your weather conditions.

VEGETABLES

Dwarf beans
Kinghorn Waxpod
Sprite
Tendergreen

Broccoli
Italian Sprouting
Purple Sprouting

Brussels sprouts
Peer Gynt
Early Button

Carrots

Leeks

Lettuce

Marrow

Welsh Onions

Petit Pois
Gullivert
Oregon Sugar Pod
Dwarf de Grace

Shallots

Spinach

Tomatoes

HERBS

Basil
Sweet
Spicy globe

Cress

Chervil

Chives

Coriander

Dill

Garlic

Mints

Marjoram

Parsley

Rosemary

Sage

Summer Savory

Tarragon

Thyme

FRUIT

Apples
Dessert
Cox's Orange Pippin
Discovery
James Grieve
Ellison's Orange
Lord Lambourne
Sunset
Egremont Russet
Orleans Reinette
Cookers
Arthur Turner
Lane's Prince Albert
Crawley Beauty
Grenadier
Encore

Pears
Doyenne du Comice
Conference
Josephine de Malines
Louise Bonne de Jersey
Winter Nelis

Cherries
Early Rivers
Waterloo
Noir de Guben

Apricots
Moor Park
New Large Early

Nectarines
Early Rivers
Lord Napier

Peaches
Peregrine
Rochester

Plums
Reine Claude
Cambridge Greengage
Victoria
Early Rivers

Currants
Boskoop Giant (black)
Seabrook's Black
Baldwin (black)
Malling Jet (black)
Laxton's No 1 (red)
White Versailles (white)

Gooseberries
Langley Gage
Lancer
Lancashire Lad
Careless

Blackberries
Parsley–leaved form

Raspberries
Malling Jewel
Malling Promise
Heritage
September
Yellow Antwerp

Strawberries
Royal Sovereign
Cambridge Late Pine
Cambridge Favourite
Red Gauntlet

Blueberries
Atlantic
Ivanhoe
Bluecrop
Early Bluejay

Rhubarb

ABOVE: *Rosemary Verey's spectacular vegetable garden at Barnsley House in Gloucestershire, England, was in part inspired by the great potager garden at the Chateau de Villandry in France. In her garden, Rosemary grows a wealth of material, including purple and green cabbages, standard rose bushes, herbs, and as well, espaliered and goblet-trained apple trees. The whole garden is segmented by brick and block paths to create narrow beds which are easy to maintain as well as providing a decorative layout.*

The white garden

So much has been written about Vita Sackville-West's famous white garden at Sissinghurst, that it must surely be one of the most widely used inspirations for similar themes in countries all around the world. The beauty of this enclosed room, which is just one part of the large walled garden she designed with her husband Harold Nicholson, has impressed people from the time of its creation and final completion in 1950.

The white garden was the last garden created at Sissinghurst. Vita's plantsmanship and her beautifully orchestrated garden schemes had already won her acclaim. She and her husband successfully devised a series of architectural shapes using the old walls of their striking sixteenth century castle and, as well, created new walls by planting trees and hedges.

White gardens are particularly beautiful at night; and in a publication printed before the Second World War, Vita first hints at her growing awareness of and fondness for this theme when she noted the beauty of some white lilies and how she was enchanted by white field daisies, luminescent in the summer dusk. The decision to design the planting scheme for the walled garden of the Priest's House, which is where they dined and entertained, was made in 1949.

Nicholson referred to this garden as the white and grey garden, and indeed these are the colours of the material contained in it.

The layout consists of a series of garden beds bordered by box and lavender. Iceberg roses are underplanted with white *Pulmonarias*, and blocks of *Nicotiana*, *Antirrhinum*, *Artemisia* and *Crambe* fill the spaces. Grey *Santolina and Achillea ageratifolia*, along with white regale lilies, add to the scene; and at the centre of the garden paths a late-blooming *Rosa longicuspis* rambles over an iron pergola.

The beauty of this garden has been maintained through the years and it must be one of the most visited gardens in England. Its layout is simple and strong, making it enjoyable whether it is viewed from within its walls or from one of the windows of the castle tower.

Developing your own version of a white garden can be fun and a great challenge. It is possible to choose a variety of plants which will flower at different times of the year thus always ensuring visual interest. If your patio or courtyard garden is located near your house, add soft lighting to create an attractive eating and entertaining area for warmer summer nights.

LEFT: The famous white garden at Sissinghurst in England attracts thousands of visitors year-round who come to enjoy the ethereal beauty of this planting scheme. Richly cultivated with silver, grey and white plants, in beds bordered by box and lavender, the garden includes Stachys lanata, Rosa 'Iceberg', Pulmonarias, *and* Nicotiana. *A silver willow-leaved pear tree is a glorious addition at one end of the garden room, and a* Rosa longicuspis *rambles over an iron pergola at the centre of the paths bisecting the garden.*

Plan for a white garden

This charming garden room has been designed to create its own walls. It provides a
beautiful space to be enjoyed during the day and especially at night when the colour and
perfumes of the flowers will enhance the surroundings. The addition of some subtle
lighting in this garden would also add to its beauty.

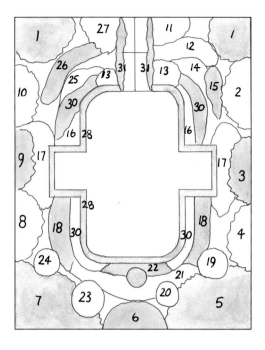

Key to planting scheme

1. *Eucryphia x nymansensis*
2. *Styrax japonica*
3. *Philadelphus* 'Belle Etoile'
4. *Magnolia sieboldii*
5. *Magnolia wilsonii*
6. *R.* 'Nevada'
7. *Cercis siliquastrum* 'Alba'
8. *Amelanchier arborea*
9. *Philadelphus* 'Burfordensis'
10. *Halesia carolina*
11. *Viburnum plicatum* 'Lanarth'
12. *Cimicifuga racemosa*
13. *Romneya coulteri*
14. *Hemerocallis*
15. *Polygonatum multiflorum*
16. *Stachys byzantina*
17. *Rosa rugosa* 'Alba'
18. *Delphinium* (white)
19. *Pieris taiwanensis*
20. *Spirea thunbergii*
21. *Hosta plantaginea*
22. *Phlox* 'Snowdrift'
23. *Zenobia pulverulenta*
24. *Viburnum carlesii*
25. *Francoa ramosa*
26. *Anemone x hybrida* 'Honorine Jobert'
27. *Syringa persica* 'Alba'

28. *Buxus sempervirens*
29. Ground cover under trees:
    Helleborus niger
    Helleborus orientalis
    Artemisia lactiflora
    Anemone nemorosa
    Cyclamen hederifolium
    Galanthus nivalis
    Erythronium spp
30. Annuals:
    Antirrhinum (white)
    Nicotiana alata
    Zinnia 'Envy'
    Pansies
    Violas
31. *Carpinus betulus*

Additional perennials:
    Astilbe x arendsii
    Achillea ptarmica 'The Pearl'
    Aster
    Bergenia 'Silberlicht'
    Campanula alliariifolia
    Convallaria majalis
    Dianthus
    Epimedium x youngeanum 'Niveum'
    Euphorbia characias 'Wulfenii'
    Paeonia
    Thalictrum aquilegifolium

This is a truly romantic garden which is both pretty and endearing. Its formal framework is planted in cottage style with an abundance of trees, shrubs, ground cover and flowers. It is designed as a small enclosed room which could easily be incorporated into a larger garden layout.

A minimum of structure is needed to contain this area and a picket fence or trellis would be adequate. Eventually the garden will not require walls at all because, with care and sufficient planting, the trees and shrubs will create their own enclosure.

To enter the garden you pass under a classical ogee arch planted with hornbeam (*Carpinus betulus*) which is pruned to create a flat tunnel. This deciduous shrub usually retains its autumn leaves until the following spring. The lawn at the centre of the layout is edged with box (*Buxus sempervirens*) hedging, and the seats on either side provide a place to sit in the morning or afternoon sun.

The central focus is the large gothic urn standing on its base surrounded by drifts of white flowers and backed by a 'Nevada' rose, which produces single, slightly blowsy flowers throughout summer and often again in the autumn. *Rosa rugosa* 'Alba' is planted behind the two seats, where its perfumed, large, pure-white flowers, and tomato-red autumn fruit can be enjoyed.

Annuals planted at the front of the garden beds add to the profusion of flowers and the underplanting of the trees is a mixture of ground cover and flowers, which ensures that there is always something of interest throughout the seasons.

This is a very livable garden, which will however require quite a lot of maintenance. Regular hoeing, replanting, feeding and watering are the keys to its success.

The colour garden

Claude Monet, the French impressionist, painted a wonderful series of pictures featuring the flowers and shrubs and, in particular, the lily ponds in his garden in the village of Giverny, near Vernon in France. He left behind not only a legacy of beautiful pictures, but also a delightful colour garden which has been restored for later generations to enjoy.

Planted with a colourful riot of seasonal material, orange and red nasturtiums, daisies, roses, *Asters*, *Ageratum* and sunflowers all take their turn to glow against the pink and green colours of the house.

Monet kept the palette of his garden deliberately light, balancing form, texture and colour for effect. His planting scheme was based on a formal layout and included standard roses and many arches over pathways to complete the structure.

In Victorian England colour was used in a different way. Captivated by the new brightly coloured flowering plants that became available, the Victorians developed a passion for flat bedding schemes using salvias, geraniums, *Calceolarias*, *Lobelias* and *Ageratum*. In direct contrast, William Robinson campaigned for change, and developed a new style of gardening where the plants were grown informally producing soft integrated patterns and textures.

Robinson's friend and compatriot, Gertrude Jekyll, was a gifted colourist who also taught the English how to use a discerning eye when planting herbaceous borders and woodland gardens. She wrote prolifically during her lifetime on the art of colour planning and planting gardens.

Choosing colours is a personal decision. However, learning to experiment with colour combinations and tints to create harmony or contrast in a garden can be a truly satisfying experience.

If you choose a number of favourite colours or just one as the basis for a scheme, this can often be the key to an harmonious garden plan. In the case of an existing property where you inherit a mixed garden plot and want to turn it into a comprehensive planting scheme, an easy way to begin is to shift or remove material which does not complement its neighbours in colour or texture.

Nature imposes some limitations on the success of the colour garden. In spring, bright-coloured bulbs can set the stage. However, their flowering period is short, and other flowers must replace them while the leaves die down and the bulb is given time to replace its nutrients for the next season.

Careful control of the range of bright spring colours used in a small courtyard or patio area is important. Planting bulbs in containers can often be the answer. This allows them to be moved around and tried out in various positions, and to be removed from view completely when their flowering season is over.

Summer brings roses, perennials and annuals in every colour and hue to be mixed and matched. When autumn arrives there are more changes to the palette, with oranges, reds and browns beginning to mark the leaves and stems of plants.

In winter, the structure of shrubs and the texture of leaves take over and play the predominant role. Planning for this season cannot be overlooked, and there are shrubs which flower and add beauty to the layout at this time. *Helleborus* are ideal, adding a gentle touch of colour; and wintersweet (*Chimonanthus praecox*), witch hazel (*Hamamelis*) and Tartarian dogwood (*Cornus alba*) are also good plants to include.

The success of a garden planted with a mix of colours or in one co-ordinated colour scheme depends on taking the demands of nature into account and on providing a framework that will stand the test of time and give an enjoyable landscape throughout all seasons.

LEFT: Claude Monet's colour garden at Giverny in France has always captivated visitors with its riot of seasonal colours. Monet's aim was to plant in dense layers leaving no patches of bare earth. In summer, the blooms of standard roses, campanulas, poppies and peonies predominate, and the green/blue steel archways which form tunnels above the paths are swathed with climbing roses of pink, red and yellow. As the season matures, dahlias, French marigolds and nasturtiums enrich the colour palette.

Plan for a nostalgic colour garden

Τhis pretty colour garden, recalling the charm of days gone by, is designed to be viewed from the terrace of a house. The focus of attention is the central sundial backed by a rose coiled around a low chain and post fence. The borders are planted in pinks on one side and blues and lemons on the other.

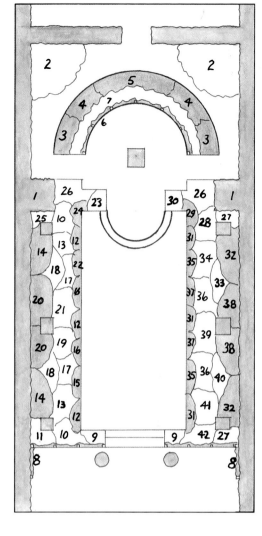

Key to planting scheme

1 *Carpinus betulus*
2 *Sorbus aria* 'Majestica'
3 *Astilbe x arendsii* (cream)
4 *Anemone x hybrida* (white)
5 *Euphorbia characias* ssp. *wulfenii*
6 *R.* 'Buff Beauty'
7 *Hosta plantaginea*
8 *R.* 'Penelope'

Pink border:
9 *Stachys byzantina*
10 *Lavatera* 'Barnsley'
11 *Lupinus* (pink)
12 *Dianthus* 'Doris'
13 *Aster* 'Harrington's Pink'
14 *Alcea* (pink)
15 *Sedum* 'Brilliant'
16 *Heuchera* 'Coral Cloud'
17 *Penstemon* 'Pink Endurance'
18 *Echinacea purpurea*
19 *Achillea* 'Cerise Queen'
20 *Phlox paniculata* (pink)

21 *Astilbe* (pink)
22 *Veronica spicata*
23 *Iris laevigata* 'Rose Queen'
24 *Geranium sanguineum* var. *striatum*
25 *Filipendula rubra*
26 *R.* 'Iceberg' (standard)

Blue/lemon border:
27 *Lupinus* (dark-blue)
28 *Aster* (mid-blue)
29 *Veronica spicata* (grey)
30 *Iris innominata*
31 *Nepeta x faassenii* 'Blue Beauty'
32 *Delphinium* 'Summer Skies'
33 *Lobelia siphilitica*
34 *Tradescantia*
35 *Penstemon heterophyllus*
36 *Achillea* 'Moonshine'
37 *Geranium* 'Buxton's Blue'
38 *Phlox paniculata* (blue)
39 *Delphinium x belladonna*
40 *Anchusa* 'Loddon Royalist'
41 *Campanula lactiflora*
42 *Thalictrum aquilegifolium*

From the terrace of the house, the eye travels into this garden past two Elizabethan jardinières, over an oblong lawn, and up two steps to the central sundial.

A hornbeam (*Carpinus betulus*) hedge, precisely clipped with wings, and with an arch cut out at the centre back to provide access to a service area, provides a solid wall of green.

The strong structure and formal layout will provide plenty of attraction all year round. The trellis obelisks, placed at regular intervals along each border, provide height to the planting scheme, and do not have plants growing over them.

The right border is a mix of blue flowering plants with lemon highlights and grey foliage around the front. On the opposite side of the lawn, bright pinks and deep strong pinks intermingle for a charming effect. Two standard 'Iceberg' roses, which flower in profusion throughout the summer, mark the end of the borders. A narrow service path at the rear of the garden beds means that hedge trimming is not difficult.

Behind the sundial, a low curved brick wall forms a background for a planting of white and cream perennials which set off the 'Buff Beauty' rose with its frilly double flowers ranging in colour from buff-yellow to almost apricot. The rose is trained to coil around the low chain and post fence in the style developed by the French.

This garden is completed with the two *Sorbus aria* 'Majestica' trees planted in the back corners. They have clusters of white cherry-blossom sized flowers, followed by masses of long-stemmed oblong fruit that ripen to scarlet.

Other perennials to plant are: *Achillea filipendulina, Agapanthus praecox, Alchemilla mollis, Anthemis tinctoria* 'E.C. Buxton', *Campanula persicifolia, Echinops, Eryngium alpinum, Euphorbia polychroma, Geranium psilostemon, Hemerocallis, Iris* (bearded), *Kniphofia, Lavendula angustifolia, Paeonia, Platycodon grandiflorus, Rudbeckia* 'Herbstonne', *Salvia patens, Scabiosa, Sisyrinchium striatum, Stokesia laevis, Thalictrum delavayi.*

The Mediterranean-style garden

Walled gardens in the hot sunny climates of Spain, Italy and Greece have an individual charm. Paved with cobblestones, on which stand huge containers planted with sun- and wind-tolerant plants, and with a water feature in their midst, they provide a sheltered retreat where meals or a drink in the shade can be enjoyed.

One of the most striking features of the Mediterranean landscape is the way that every available piece of land is used to grow vines and crops or to provide an outdoor garden area for the house. Hillsides are terraced, and the colour palette is rich with greens and browns — layered one on the other — to provide unity and harmony in often very small

LEFT: This Mediterranean-style garden incorporates a very effective use of pebble paving. It was designed for the Chelsea Garden Show which is an annual event in London. Two palms (Sabal), in terracotta pots, dominate the planting scheme of lilies (Lilium), box hedging (Buxus sempervirens), and convolvulus (Convolvulus cneorum).

areas. Creepers are grown to clothe the walls and terraces. Terracotta tiles and bricks mark out the layout and structure. Rows of brightly coloured geraniums or pelargoniums often line the edge of the paths and adorn windowsills, or provide a low fence to mark out an area for eating. Citrus fruits are grown in larger pots, and clipped green shrubs — chosen for their rich colour and dense foliage — mark boundaries and border driveways.

Sun, wind and water are major influences on gardens around the world. When the early colonists settled new lands they were faced with a range of climatic conditions often very different from those in their original homelands. People who found themselves in subtropical regions, had to change their ideas radically about the type of garden they would create around their homes, and many gardens in the Mediterranean tradition evolved.

The courtyard or patio garden is invariably an extension of the house rather than a separate entity. The layout is generally formal with very few bedded plants. Flowers are added in containers so

that they can be moved around or taken away when the blooms are finished. Sculpture and classical vases and urns are frequently displayed within the format.

Water plays a major role and every conceivable form of water feature can be found in Mediterranean-style gardens, such as central or walled fountains and interconnecting pools, or simply a birdbath. Planting schemes are primarily in green, which helps to create a feeling of coolness when the sun is at its hottest. A pergola or vine-covered arbour, with a table beneath it for meals, is usually incorporated.

In many cities and small villages throughout Europe it is possible to wander for miles along narrow streets glimpsing small family courtyards or patios through the gates and doors set into the surrounding walls.

Peristyle courtyards are also a feature of many older inner city apartment blocks in the ancient metropolises of Rome, Florence, Athens and Madrid. They are oases of quiet enjoyment and tranquillity amidst the noise and chaos of traffic and city streets.

The Mediterranean-style garden

This extremely simple courtyard or patio design for a Mediterranean style garden
is enhanced by the careful use of interesting paving materials in gentle shades of terracotta
and pink. The minimum of planting and the adaptability of the space makes it an
ideal low-maintenance project.

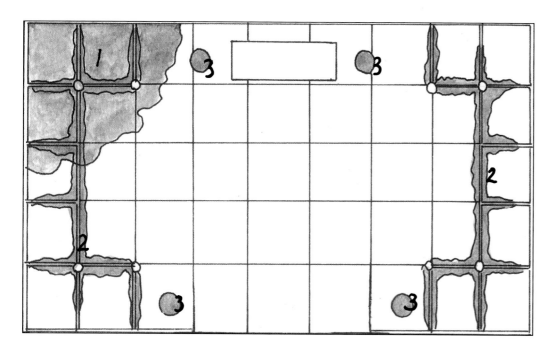

This extremely simple and elegant design provides the maximum flexibility in living space and relies on a large open area and classical French urns as the focal points. Because the emphasis on form rather than planting makes for minimal upkeep, it would work equally well as an enclosed city garden or as a design for a roof garden.

The total space has been divided into a grid pattern. The flooring consists of squares of creamy-pink pea gravel contained by brick edging. The walls are plastered and are a soft colour to complement the terracotta bricks. Planting is limited to a tree overshadowing one corner and the French urns full of annuals are changed to match the seasons. More pots of plants could be included, but they should be limited to simple shapes and to one type only, to complement the simplicity of the design.

A pergola, in the same grid pattern as the paving, and constructed of simple circular columns and timber framing, is designed to shade each end of the garden. For extra shade, a *Wisteria venusta* with its fragrant white flowers is used as a light covering over the pergola, and should be hard pruned to keep it from smothering the structure.

A multi-trunked strawberry tree (*Arbutus x andrachnoides*) planted in one corner has attractive peeling cinnamon-red bark, and as it flowers in late autumn and winter, it adds an area of interest during the colder months.

A change of level, to increase the feeling of space, has been achieved by dropping the central paving one step. An alternative idea, if an area like this was wanted more to look out on than to use, would be to include a simple rectangular reflection pool.

Overall, this is a gentle and harmonious modern design that would suit a number of situations. As well, it offers an easy-care solution to an outdoor area.

PLANTS FOR THE COURTYARD & PATIO

Choosing plants

Taking care to choose quality plants for the courtyard or patio is most important. In smaller enclosed spaces everything is on view all year and must contribute to an overall scheme.

Personal preference always plays a part in designing and planting any garden, and everyone has their own favourites. The plants included here are all worth a place in any garden, although you should check what will perform best in your own particular climate zone before making a final buying decision.

Trees and shrubs have been chosen for their good foliage and form, as much as for their flowers. Those which could be difficult to grow have been avoided. The shrubs, also, have been chosen for their good foliage and, where applicable, because they flower over as long a season as possible. Plants that have a tendency to become coarse and need constant cutting back have been avoided.

The perennials, generally, have been selected for their ability to withstand some shade as this is essential in all but the most open sunny gardens.

TREES

Key
AC	Autumn colour
E	Evergreen
D	Deciduous
*	Topiary

Acer palmatum (maple) D AC
Good foliage, small trees
griseum
Attractive bark
circinatum
Wine and white flowers
davidii
Attractive bark
pennsylvanicum
Attractive bark

Amelanchier arborea D AC
Attractive white flowers, early spring

Arbutus x andrachnoides E
Cinnamon bark, attractive clusters of white flowers; strawberry-like fruit
menziesii E
Attractive clusters of white flowers late spring, strawberry-like fruit

Betula pendula (silver birch or European white birch) D AC
White trunk, delicate foliage; Slender woodland tree

Carpinus betulus (hornbeam) D AC
Grey fluted bark, good hedging, leaves retained into winter

Cercis siliquastrum 'Alba' (judas tree) D
Heart-shaped leaves, pea-flowers in spring

Cladrastris lutea AC
Wisteria-like, fragrant flowers, good foliage

Cotoneaster frigidus 'Cornubia' D
Spectacular crimson fruit

LEFT: A burst of golden daffodils above the rich purples and variegated green leaves of Pulmonaria, *wood anemone and* Aster frikartii *greets the new spring season. Designed by Susan Whittington.*

PREVIOUS PAGE: This wall has been planted with a climbing Tea rose and a single white hybrid Clematis *to offer a brilliant display of colour and texture.*

TREES (Continued)

Cornus mas (dogwood) D AC
Small yellow winter flowers, bright red fruit
> *kousa* 'Chinensis' D AC
> Elegant form, white bracts in spring, strawberry-like fruits

Crataegus x lavallei 'Carrierei' D
Orange-red fruits against dark foliage
> *phaenopyrum* D AC
> Crimson fruits
> *pinnatifida* 'Major' D AC
> Bold leaves, crimson fruits
> *punctata* D
> White blossom, crimson fruits

Eucryphyia x nymansensis E
Large white summer flowers

Euonymus europaeus 'Red Cascade' (spindle) D AC
Scarlet fruit

Gleditsia triacanthos (honey locust)
Good foliage, seed pods

Halesia carolina (snowdrop tree) D
Bell-shaped flowers in spring
> *monticola* D
> Larger tree, bell flowers

Ilex aquifolium (green-leaved forms) (holly) E *
Fine foliage, red berries in winter

Laburnum x watereri D
Yellow chains of flowers in spring

Laurus nobilis (bay tree) E *
Good foliage

Magnolia denudata
Early cream goblet flowers
> *soulangeana* 'Lennei Alba'
> Later, larger cream flowers
> *wilsonii*
> White cupped flowers, summer

Malus spectabilis (crab apple) D
Red buds, open blush
> *floribunda* D
> Early blossom, red buds, open white

> *coronaria* 'Charlottae' D AC
> Double pink, flowers late

Prunus 'Okame' D AC
Deep pink bells, spring
> *sargentii* 'Accolade' D AC
> Attractive dark bark, single pink flowers
> *serrula* D
> Brown shiny bark, small white flowers
> *serrulata* 'Hokusai' D AC
> Semi-double, pale-pink flowers; spreading tree
> 'Shirotae' D AC
> Small tree, spreading; single white flowers
> 'Tai Haku' D AC
> Big white flowers, coppery new leaves

Pyrus salicifolia 'Pendula' (silver weeping pear) D
Beautiful form and foliage

Quercus ilex (holm oak) E *
Grey-green foliage

Rhus typhina 'Laciniata' D AC
Fine cut leaves

Sorbus alnifolia D AC
Bright red fruits
> *aria* 'Majestica' (whitebeam) D AC
> Grey leaves, crimson fruits
> *aucuparia* (rowan) D
> Red berries
> 'Joseph Rock' D AC
> Yellow-amber fruits
> *sargentiana* D AC
> Large leaves, scarlet fruit
> *cashmiriana* D
> Pink flowers, white fruit

Stuartia sinensis D AC
Attractive bark, small camellia-like flowers, fragrant, white
> *pseudocamellia* D
> Attractive bark, white flowers, yellow anthers

Styrax japonica D
Dainty white bells, summer
> *obassia* D
> Handsome leaves, good bark, white bells, summer

ABOVE: The stored warmth from this brick wall provides an ideal place to train espaliered fruit trees. This peach tree is savouring the benefits of the warm situation and has produced a magnificent crop of fruit.

BULBS

Key

W   Woodland (as ground cover)

Allium
Ornamental onion flowers

Anemone blanda (woodland anemone)
W Blue or white flowers
    nemorosa
      W Blue or white flowers
    coronaria 'de Caen' (florists anemone)
      Red, white or blue poppies, spring

Cyclamen hederifolium W
Attractive marbled leaves, pink or white flowers, autumn

Daffodils, esp *poeticus*
forms large flowers, variety of colours

Eranthis hyemalis (aconite) W
Yellow flowers early spring, naturalises in shade

Erythronium spp (dog's tooth violet) W
Cream or yellow flowers, marbled leaves

Galanthus nivalis (English snowdrop) W
Naturalises well in shade

Galtonia candicans (summer hyacinth)
Tall white bells in summer

Hyacinthoides hispanica (Spanish bluebells)
Blue giant form for shade

SHRUBS

Key

AC	Autumn colour
D	Deciduous
Dw	Dwarf
E	Evergreen
M	Medium
T	Tall
*	Topiary
**	Espaliered
W	Woodland garden

Acer japonicum 'Aconitifolium' (maple) D AC M
Finely cut leaves, red flowers

Aesculus parviflora (dwarf horse chestnut) D AC W
White flowers, summer

Aucuba japonica (green-leaved forms) E M
Large glossy, green leaves, red berries

Rhododendron (azalea)
   Ghent hybrids D W M
   Fragrant, yellow-oranges, white
   Knap Hill hybrids D W M
   Mollis hybrids D W M
   Mucronatum 'Album' E W Dw
   Large white perfumed flowers

   Occidentale hybrids D W M
   Fragrant, pink

Berberis darwinii (barberry) E
Dark foliage, deep golden flowers, plum-coloured fruit
   gagnepainii E
   Yellow flowers, black berries
   linearifolia E M
   Orange-red flowers
   x stenophylla E M
   Yellow flowers, long graceful branches
   jamesiana D AC L
   Yellow flowers, coral-red berries

Buddleia davidii hybrids E M
Fragrant flowers, attractive to butterflies, summer

Buxus sempervirens (English box) E Dw *
Tight, dark-green foliage

Camellia japonica varieties E
Fine bold foliage, varied colours, flowers winter
   sasanqua E M **
   Smaller informal blooms, autumn
   x saluenensis E
   Large flowers, good foliage

SHRUBS (continued)

Ceanothus x delinianus 'Gloire de Versailles' D M
Soft blue summer flowers
      'Delight' E M
      Rich blue spring flowers
      'Burkwoodii' E M
      Rich blue flowers, summer–autumn
      'Autumn Blue' E M
      Rich dark-blue flowers, summer–autumn

Chaenomeles speciosa hybrids (japonica, ornamental quince) D **
Early spring flowers

Chimonanthus praecox (wintersweet) D T **
Fragrant waxy yellow flowers, winter

Chionanthus retusus (fringe tree) D
White flowers, summer
      virginicus D
      White flowers, spectacular display

Choisya ternata E M
Glossy foliage, fragrant white flowers

Cotoneaster affinis var. *bacillaris* D
Large shrub. White arching sprays, red fruit
      bullatus D T
      Brilliant red fruit

Daphne x burkwoodii E Dw
Pale-pink fragrant flowers
      cneorum E Dw
      Rose-pink flowers, prostrate habit
      laureola E Dw
      Shiny foliage. Yellow-green fragrant flowers
      pontica E Dw
      Bright green glossy leaves. Fragrant yellow-green flowers

Deutzia longifolia D M
Large clusters of white or pink tinted flowers, summer
      x magnifica 'Longipetala' D M
      White clusters, summer
      scabra 'Candidissima' D T
      White double flowers

Enkianthus campanulatus D AC
Clusters of white flowers, spring

Escallonia hybrids E M **
Summer, early autumn flowers

Fatsia japonica E M
Bold leaves, black berries

Garrya elliptica E M **
Long grey-green catkins

Hamamelis mollis (witch hazel) D AC
Fragrant yellow winter flowers

Hydrangea, Lacecap varieties D M
Informal, flattened flower heads, summer
      quercifolia D M
      Attractive foliage, green flowers, summer
      serrata hybrids D Dw
      Lacecap flowers, summer

Hypericum calycinum E Dw W
Large golden flowers. Good shade ground cover
      'Hidcote' E M
      Golden-yellow flowers, summer–autumn

Ilex cornuta (holly) E M
Bold shiny leaves
      pernyi E
      Distinctive foliage, red berries

Jasminum nudiflorum (winter jasmine) D
Yellow flowers, mid-winter

Lavandula angustifolia (English lavender)
Fragrant spikes, summer

Magnolia stellata (star magnolia) D
Starry white flowers, long flowering period winter–spring
      sieboldii D
      Fragrant cup-shaped flowers, summer

Mahonia aquifolium (Oregon grape) E
Yellow flowers, early spring, attractive black berries
      'Charity' E
      Larger form, fragrant yellow flowers, autumn–winter

Nandina domestica (Chinese sacred bamboo) E
Attractive red-tinged leaves, white flowers, summer

Olearia x scilloniensis E
Grey-green leaves, white daisies, spring

SHRUBS (continued)

Osmanthus heterophyllus E
Holly-like leaves, white perfumed flowers, autumn

Paeonia lutea var. *Ludlowii* (tree peony) D
Large yellow flowers, spring, finely cut leaves

Philadelphus lemoinei hybrids (mock orange) D
White fragrant flowers, summer

Pieris formosa 'Wakehurst' (lily-of-the-valley bush) E
White flowers, spring, new growth coppery
    taiwanensis
      Earlier white flowers, coppery new growth

Potentilla fruticosa varieties D
Yellow or white flowers, summer

Prunus laurocerasus (cherry laurel) E
Bold foliage, dark shining green

Prunus Lusitanica (Portugal laurel) *
Dense dark-green foliage, white flowers

Rhododendron hybrids E
Variable bold leaves. Large rounded flower heads, spring

Romneya coulteri (Californian tree poppy)
Large white poppies over deeply-cut leaves

Rubus 'Tridel' D
Large white flowers, arching branches
    deliciosus
      Attractive bark, large white flowers
    odoratus
      Large velvety leaves, purplish-rose flowers, summer
    thibetanus
      Attractive stems, ferny leaves. Black or red fruit

Senecio x greyii E
Grey foliage. Yellow daisy flowers

Syringa persica 'Alba' (Persian lilac) D
Fragrant lilac flowers
    villosa D
      Bold foliage, lilac-rose flowers

Skimmia japonica E Dw
White flowers followed by red fruits

Spiraea 'Arguta' (bridal wreath) D
Pure white flowers, arching growth
    thunbergii D
      Earlier white flowers
    trichocarpa D
      White flowers, summer

Taxus baccata (yew) E *
Suitable hedges, shade

Vaccinium ovatum E
Dark-green leaves, coppery new growth. White or pink
bells, red berries
      corymbosum (highbush blueberry) D AC
        Pink or white flowers, attractive edible fruit

Viburnum x bodnantense D
Perfumed pink flowers, winter
    'Anne Russell' D
      Pink fragrant flowers
    carlesii D AC
      Highly perfumed white flowers
    davidii E Dw
      Leathery leaves, blue berries
    farreri D
      White fragrant flowers, winter
    plicatum 'Lanarth' D
      White lacecap flowers
    rhytidophyllum E
      Cream flowers, bold leaves
    tinus hybrids E
      Dark glossy green foliage. Pink flowers, winter

Wisteria venusta
Fragrant, white flowers yellow markings

Zenobia pulverulenta D
Lily-of-the-valley type flowers

LEFT: A glorious display of peony roses (Paeonia) has been established in this traditional walled garden. These perennials thrive in a sunny or partly shaded corner, but require a deep, rich soil. To complement their rich colours catmint (Nepeta x faassenii), purple Allium, Delphinium and white lilies (lilium) are grown.

PERENNIALS

Key

AC	Autumn colour
Dw	Dwarf
T	Tall

Acanthus spinosus
Bold leaves, tall mauve and white flowers

Achillea 'Moonshine' (yarrow)
Sulphur heads in summer
      'Cerise Queen'
      Flat flowerheads over ferny foliage
      ptarmica 'The Pearl' (boule de neige)
      Masses of double flowers

Aconitum nepellus (monkshood)
Spikes of varying blue flowers; poisonous

Alcea (hollyhock) Tall spires, distinguished

Alchemilla mollis (lady's mantle) Dw
Rounded furry foliage, greeny- yellow sprays of flowers

Anchusa azurea 'Loddon Royalist' (Italian bugloss)
Giant blue flowers

Anemone x hybrida T
Attractive cut leaves, pink or white flowers in autumn

Anthemis tinctoria
Yellow or suphur daisies

Aquilegia vulgaris (granny bonnets or columbines)
Dainty spurred flowers spring and summer

Artemisia lactiflora T
Good foliage, creamy plumes late summer

Aster (Michaelmas daisy)
Various coloured daisies, summer–autumn

Astilbe x arendsii
Finely cut foliage, summer plumes in pinks, white and red

Bergenia cordifolia and hybrids Dw
Bold evergreen foliage, pink, red or white flowers, spring

Campanula alliariifolia
Slender spikes of delicate bells
      persicifolia
      Summer flowers of white or blue

      lactiflora T
      Pale-blue summer flowers
      latifolia T
      Purple or white flowers, autumn

Cimicifuga racemosa T
Finely cut foliage, cream spikes, summer

Delphinium varieties
Tall spikes of blue, white or pink

Echinacea purpurea (coneflower)
Tall daisies, late summer

Echinops (globe thistle)
Grey spiny foliage, metallic blue

Epimedium grandiflorum Dw
Good foliage, various coloured flowers, spring

Eryngium alpinum (sea holly)
Grey-green foliage, metallic blue flowers, summer

Euphorbia amygdaloides var. *robbiae* (wood spurge)
Good foliage, greeny flowers
      characias ssp. *wulfenii*
      Grey-green foliage
      polychroma
      Bright yellow flowers

Filipendula rubra
Plumes of flowers, handsome lobed leaves

Francoa appendiculata (may) *F. ramosa*
Tall dainty spikes, pink or white

Geranium endressii (cranesbill) Dw
Pink flowers, spring
      'Buxton's Blue' Dw
      Blue flowers, summer
      'Johnson's Blue' Dw
      Blue flowers, summer
      pratense (meadow cranesbill)
      Violet-blue flowers
      psilostemon AC
      Pink flowers, cut leaves
      sanguineum var. *striatum*
      Veined pink flowers

ABOVE: A lovely intermingling of textures and colours in a corner of a well-stocked city garden features a hybrid perpetual shrub rose,
Bellis perennis, Euphorbia, Hosta, *a variegated tall bearded iris and* Alchemilla.

PERENNIALS *(continued)*

Helleborus orientalis (Lenten rose)
Good evergreen foliage, long lasting flowers
> *foetidus*
> Clusters of small green flowers
> *niger*
> Large waxy pink or white flowers
> *argutifolius*
> Cut leaves, bright green flowers

Hemerocallis (day lily)
Variety of colours, broad grass-like leaves

Heuchera x brizoides
hybrids (coral bells) Tall sprays of pink flowers, summer

Hosta (plantain lily)
Bold foliage, purple, lavender or white flowers, summer

Lavandula angustifolia (English lavender)
Slender, aromatic

Liriope muscari (turf lily) Dw
Purple flowers, autumn

Lupinus (lupin)
hybrids Range of colours

Macleaya cordata T
Grey cut foliage, tall brown plumes, autumn

Nepeta x faassenii (catmint)
Rich mauve flowers

Omphalodes cappadocica Dw
Brilliant blue flowers, early spring

Paeonia (peony)
Various pink, white, red summer flowers

Penstemon 'Pink Endurance'
Tubular pink flowers, summer
> *heterophyllus* Dw
> Electric-blue flowers, summer

Phlox paniculata
White, pink, purple, blue cone-shaped flowers, summer

Platycodon grandiflorus (balloon flower)
Bell-shaped flowers, blue-grey leaves

Polygonatum multiflorum (Solomon's seal)
Small white bells, arching stems, spring

Primula vulgaris (English primrose) Dw
Clusters of lemon flowers, early spring

Pulmonaria angustifolia (lungwort) Dw
Blue flowers, spring
> *saccharata* Dw
> Spotted leaves, pink and blue flowers

Rudbeckia 'Herbstonne'
Tall gold daisies, late summer

Scabiosa (scabious)
Violet-blue flowers, summer

Sedum
Flat flowerheads over long period of autumn

Sisyrinchium striatum
Cream spikes, stiff grassy foliage

Stachys byzantina (lamb's ears)
Grey leaves, small lavender flowers, summer

Stokesia laevis
Cornflower-like flowers, summer

Thalictrum aquilegifolium (meadow rue)
Dainty foliage, tall lavender or white flowers, summer
> *delavayi*
> Lilac flowers, summer
> *flavum*
> Grey-green leaves, tall yellow stems, summer

Veronica spicata (speedwell)
Spikes of flowers in summer

LEFT: This rich herbaceous border features a variety of complementary plants, including the beautiful, hardy mock orange (Philadelphus), silver-leaved lavender, lady's mantle (Alchemilla mollis), and catmint (Nepeta x faassenii). In the foreground small terracotta pots have been included to add to the overall effect. Designed by Sue Berge.

ABOVE: Here Clematis 'Henryii' lifts its starry-shaped petals to catch the sun. Rosa 'Iceberg', with its glorious semi-double flowers and mid-green foliage, acts as a stunning accompanist. Both plants enjoy growing in a rich, fertile, well-drained loam. The clematis, which does not have the ability to cling on its own, will make full use of the rose for support.

RIGHT: A rose of quiet elegance, 'Apricot Nectar' develops clusters of large, cup-shaped flowers with a good perfume. It has dark glossy foliage to complement the buff-yellow and apricot blooms.

ROSES

'Apricot Nectar' Buff-yellow and apricot
'Canary Bird' Yellow, ferny leaves, arching stems
'Chanelle' Pink to apricot
'Cream Delight' Cream-centred apricot
'French Lace' Ivory, scented
'Frühlingsanfang' Pure white, prominent stamens
'Frühlingsgold' Creamy-yellow
'Grüss an Aachen' Apricot-pink to cream
'Iceberg' White, semi-double
'Julia's Rose' Coppery fawn and cream
'Margaret Merril' Creamy white, fragrant
'Nancy Steen' Salmon pink and cream
'Nevada' Creamy white
'Penelope' Cream to apricot

'Prosperity' Double creamy white
R. rugosa 'Alba' White fragrant
R. moyesii 'Geranium' Red, attractive hips

Climbers

'Alchemist' Apricot, scented
'Alister Stella Gray' Clusters of yellow to cream
'Buff Beauty Apricot-yellow, free-flowering, scented
'Céline Forestier' Pale-primrose, recurrent
'Cloth of Gold' Creamy yellow
'Desprez à Fleurs Jaunes' Lemon, scented
'Gloire de Dijon' Double buff, recurrent
'Graham Thomas' Double yellow, scented
'Maréchal Niel' Pale-gold, scented

GROUND COVER (SHADE-TOLERANT)

Key
AC   Autumn colour
E   Evergreen
P   Perennial

Ajuga reptans E
Coppery leaves, blue flowers, spring

Alchemilla mollis (lady's mantle) E
Furry leaves, lime-yellow flowers, summer

Arctostaphylos 'Emerald Carpet' (shrub) E
Dense, fine foliage

Brunnera macrophylia (perennial forget-me-not) P
Intense blue flowers

Campanula portenschlagiana
Blue flowers, spring

Convallaria majalis (lily-of-the-valley)
Pretty bell flowers

Cotoneaster dammeri
Spreading habit, red berries, autumn

Epimedium grandiflorum
Attractively marbled leaves, yellow-orange or white flowers, early spring
      x youngeanum 'Niveum'
      Delicate flowers, spring

Geranium macrorrhizum E AC
Magenta flowers, summer
      endressii
      Pink veined flowers, low carpeter
      pratense
      Taller blue flowers, summer

Hedera helix (ivy) E
Leaves of various forms and colours

Helxine soleirolii (baby's tears)
Tiny bright green leaves

Hosta
Bold leaves, white or lavender flowers

Hypericum calycinum
Yellow flowers for dry shade

Pachysandra terminalis E
Good foliage, white flowers

Rubus tricolor E
Arching growth, white flowers, summer

Tellima grandiflora E
Attractive foliage, cream flowers

Tiarella cordifolia (foam flower) E AC
Profuse white flowers, spring–summer

Tolmiea menziesii E
Tiny green bells in spring

ANNUALS AND BIENNIALS

Ammi major (Queen Anne's lace)
Tall white flowers, summer

Antirrhinum majus (snapdragon)
Big bell flowers

Campanula medium (Canterbury bells)
Big bell flowers, spring
      alliariifolia
      Slender spike, delicate bells
      Chrysanthemum parthenium
      Clouds of small double daisies

Consolda ambigua (larkspurs)
Tall delphinium-like spikes

Cosmos
Daisy flowers in summer, finely cut leaves, cut flower

Cynoglossum amabile
Giant blue forget-me-not

Digitalis purpurea 'Alba' (foxglove)
White spires early summer

ANNUALS AND BIENNIALS (Continued)

Impatiens walleriana (busy Lizzies)
Masses of varied coloured flowers, summer

Lavatera trimestris 'Mont Blanc' (white mallow),
    'Silver Cup' (pink mallow)
    'Barnsley'
    Large bushes, good cut flower

Lobelia
Clumps of intense blue

Myosotis (forget-me-not)
Blue flowers, good in shade

Nicotiana alata (tobacco flower)
Perfumed white or pink flowers, summer
   langsdorfii
    Masses of small green bells

Nigella damascena (love-in-a-mist)
Filigree foliage, cornflower-blue flowers

Pansy
Variety of colours, long flowering

Papaver nudicaule (Iceland poppy)
Good cut flower
   Rhoeas (Shirley Poppy)
    Taller poppies, pink, white, red

Petunia
Trailing forms will stand a little shade

Primula vulgaris hybrids and *Polyanthus*
Flower from early spring
   malacoides
    Furry leaves, white or lavender spikes

Reseda alba (mignonette)
Cut flower, cream spikes

Salpiglossis sinuata
Beautifully marked flowers, mainly yellows, browns

Salvia horminum (Clary sage)
Pink or blue flowers on compact bush
   farinacea
    Tall spikes of blue or white
   patens
    Various blue forms, late summer spikes

Tradescantia (spiderwort)
Purplish-blue, white, verging to crimson

Verbena x hybrida
Trailing habit, summer flowers

Viola
Small growing, flowers for months

Viscaria
Tall grassy leaves, blue, mauve, purple flowers

Zinnia 'Envy'
Green flowers, good for cutting

PAVING PLANTS (MAINLY FOR SUNNY AREAS. ALL EVERGREEN)

Aurinia saxatilis
Grey foliage, bright yellow flowers

Armeria (thrift)
Grassy foliage

Aubrieta
Purple or pink flowers in spring

Campanula
Small growing varieties. Blue or white bell flowers, spring and summer

Cerastium tomentosum (snow in summer)
Masses of pure white flowers over grey leaves

Cotula reptans
Finely cut foliage, often bronzy

Dianthus (pink)
Grey foliage, often scented flowers

Phlox subulata
Pink, white or blue flowers, summer

Viola 'Maggie Mott'
Extended flowering through colder months

DECORATIVE FEATURES

The Finishing Touches

Often it is the finishing touches, the accessories, that change a room from the mundane into a striking environment. Like a room, a courtyard or patio is fundamentally a space that must be planned, decorated and furnished with an eye to structure, colour, balance, scale and use.

From early times, garden ornaments have been used to adorn the courtyard or patio. The Romans left a rich treasure-trove of classical statues and urns for later generations to use in their gardens. The French followed this approach and made use of vistas and focal points to frame special features such as fountains, containers and statues. Later, gardens in Europe and in the United Kingdom featured statues, sculpture and planting containers, as well as pergolas, trellis work, arbours and summerhouses.

There are many public and private gardens throughout the world today in which good examples of special features can be seen. English gardens in particular include lovely examples of the use of statues and vases. In America, a fine example of the harmonious blending of sculpture and plants can be seen at Jasmine Hill, Alabama; and in Maryland, the owner of the Ladew Gardens has made good use of topiary as the main theme.

Today, we have a variety to choose from, such as antique garden ornaments, excellent reproduction material, and

ABOVE: In this interesting garden planted with Santolina, statice (Limonium), and lavender, the illusion of a larger landscape extending beyond the walls has been created by the trompe-l'oeil painting. This stylish and centuries-old art form is currently enjoying a much deserved revival.

LEFT: Choosing an ornament to adorn a garden can often be the final creative touch to complete the picture. This small stone statue of a child looks delightful surrounded by a froth of roses, columbines and Mexican daisies (Erigeron). Designed by Gail Jenkins.

PREVIOUS PAGE: The perfect home was found for this pair of lovers by creating a niche in the hedge for them to repose in.

modern sculptures. A special piece selected carefully for scale will enhance a garden's design and give great pleasure.

FOUNTAINS, MASKS AND POOLS

A fountain or small ornamental pool is often the focus of a larger geometric layout. In smaller enclosed gardens the wall fountain, featuring a heraldic head or mask, can be used as a method of pouring water into a basin or pool.

The fountain owes its origins to the classical gardens created by the Romans. The Italians later developed elaborate water spectacles in their gardens, with the Terrace of a Hundred Fountains at the Villa d'Este being the most spectacular. The mechanics of providing an adequate water supply were sometimes extremely involved. For example, hydraulic pumps were used by the French to feed the fountains and water canals at Versailles.

Today, fountain designs vary greatly in style, and range from the traditional to the contemporary. Reproductions of the classical shapes are available in a variety of natural materials. A small electric pump can be used to pump water to a garden fountain and control the level at which it plays. If this type of feature is included, it is important to consider the effect wind will have on the water, as even a light breeze can spread spray over a distance.

The wall fountain is a stone or metal spout which forces water to gush swiftly from a narrow pipe into a small pool or basin. Spouts can be very attractive features, with the face or mask usually depicting a human or an animal form. Two lovely examples can be seen in England. One is at Hazelbury Manor in Wiltshire, where a delightful antique Italian lead fountain mask has been set into a wall above a square pool containing variegated Koi carp. The other is at Kingcombe in Gloucestershire, where someone with a delightful sense of humour has made a carving of Sir Gordon Russell—an owner of the property—with his glasses perched on the end of his nose and water gushing from his mouth.

Small ornamental pools have appeared in enclosed gardens throughout history. Early Persian paradise gardens, whose influence spread to India, North Africa and Spain, were divided into four symbolic segments with a water tank in the centre. This style has been used in every country where buildings are constructed around a square courtyard or patio.

To include a small pool in a garden today is not difficult. However, getting the size, position and shape right demands very careful planning. Many preformed shapes are available, as well as

ABOVE: A mask of a lion set in a brick wall makes an interesting water spout above a small stone sink filled with pebbles. Designed by Anthony Noel.

flexible pool liners. Colour selection is very important as the pool should blend in with the environment and look as natural as possible.

The pool can be set into the ground or raised with an edge to create a comfortable seat. Take care with the details of the surround. Tiles can crack in severe frosts and their shiny appearance is often difficult to handle aesthetically. More natural coloured materials and finishes are easier to incorporate into the design.

STATUES

Careful consideration and restraint are the rules for including statues or sculpture in the enclosed garden. There are many delightful antique, modern, and reproduction pieces on the market, but finally, style is a very personal matter.

The positioning of a statue within the garden is always important. The easiest way to include a good piece is to design the garden around what you have in mind. If you see something you think you would like to incorporate into an already established garden, cut out a polystyrene shape of it and try it in various positions before you finally decide.

Normally, statues work best as a focal point, in an alcove, or as a surprise around a corner. The simple classical styles are more enduring. A piece of sculpture is, after all, on display twelve months of the year, year after year. Stone balls, obelisks, finials and sundials are all classic pieces worth considering.

If your ornament is new and you want to give it an aged look as quickly as possible, try pouring sour milk on it to hasten the process.

ABOVE: This beautifully detailed stone statue of a woman enjoys a tranquil setting surrounded by trees and shrubs. Before buying a large piece of statuary or sculpture for the garden, give careful consideration to its location and the affect it will create not only in summer but also in winter when many plants will have little or no foliage.

VASES AND URNS

Vases and urns have always been popular in the enclosed garden. Used as a centre-piece in some designs or set at regular intervals to mark out a square or rectangular format, they have been recorded as a device from the earliest times in Greek and Roman peristyle courtyards.

Early copies of the classical Roman designs were made in marble and stone. Later, they were cast in metal, notably bronze and lead. A successful less costly product developed in Britain—Coade stone ware—proved to be more resistant to weathering than many quarried stones.

From the end of the eighteenth century, artificial stone was used in addition to well-fired ceramic ware. By 1850, cast iron had become the common material. Today, vases and urns are cast in artificial stone, modelled in terracotta, and are also available in a range of shapes in plastic and fibreglass.

The decision to include these objects depends on individual taste and whether there is a place in the garden for them. Scale is all-important. Avoid dotting various examples around a courtyard or patio, as this can be disastrous. Look for quality and good detailing on any items you are contemplating buying.

BIRDHOUSES AND BIRDBATHS

These delightful objects have appeared in a variety of guises ranging from the most traditional to the contemporary.

Birds can be attracted to the garden by the addition of a simple feeding table or a birdbath to provide water for drinking and bathing. More elaborate birdhouses can be bought, but a simple homemade variety, prettily decorated and hung in a tree, can be equally effective. A traditional dovecote does not need to be huge and will provide an attractive feature where space permits.

Make sure that the design of any house, table or bath attracts the birds but also protects them from neighbourhood cats.

LEFT: A selection of simple garden flowers has been chosen to fill this handsomely carved vase which would make a classic addition to most traditional gardens.

RIGHT: Birdhouses always seem to add a style and charm of their own to a garden. Here, three doll-like houses have been mounted on poles and used like a piece of sculpture to mark the end of a garden walk. The doves, strutting on the grass below, are the lucky inhabitants.

ABOVE: In this formal garden, a new gazebo has been designed to complement the layout and the architecture of the surrounding houses. Its location, proportions, and interesting use of trellis for the walling, all add to the garden's overall charm and well-furnished appearance.

GARDEN BUILDINGS
THE GAZEBO AND SUMMERHOUSE

Designing a charming gazebo, or a summerhouse, or even a garden shed for storing essential pots and tools, should bring forth all your imaginative skills. A simple trellis structure overgrown with a beautiful Kiftsgate rose, or a rustic thatch-roofed summerhouse, can become a major feature in an enclosed garden.

Garden buildings draw on a range of historical styles. Deciding on the right structure to include will be dictated by the architecture of the house and its scale, materials and effect.

A gazebo or summerhouse is a small building, which can be either free-standing or attached to a wall. The traditional gazebo has a reasonably steeply pitched roof, which is sometimes adorned with turrets and scalloped detailing. It is possible, however, to design a beautifully proportioned flat-roofed summerhouse if this suits the garden and surrounding architecture better.

We generally include a gazebo to have somewhere to sit in the sun but out of the breeze. If space permits, the addition of a table and chairs can make this a charming outside eating room.

If you want something unique and individual you could commission an artist to decorate your summerhouse or folly. Classic examples are often circular in plan with six or eight stone columns supporting a domed roof. The inside of the dome is then painted with a *trompe l'oeil* clouded sky, and sometimes the columns are finished to look like marble.

Where a more utilitarian building is required in a courtyard or patio to house gardening apparatus, it is essential that the design is creative, blending in with the qualities of the area, or that the construction is concealed in a tangle of beautiful ramblers and climbers. Alternatively, the design could incorporate a secret room out the back to store all the bits and pieces from view; or a layout could be used where all the working material is on display—in immaculate order and lined up with precision.

THE CONSERVATORY

Conservatories are useful as a structure linking the house to the garden, or can be incorporated as a small free-standing structure or attached to a garden room.

Originally, conservatories were built to provide a stable environment for the propagation and growth of plants that would not flourish in the natural environment. They became popular in the Regency and Victorian periods when glass was first mass-produced.

They can provide a charming outdoor/indoor room; and, if they have a concrete floor and are attached to the house, they can be used to store solar energy which will assist with heating the home in the evening. A conservatory is also an ideal place to winter-over less hardy specimen plants from the garden.

There are many designs for conservatories, and they should be considered in relationship to the design of the residence. Glass, if clean, can reflect the planting around it. It also reflects sunlight, and therefore should be located so that problems of dazzling reflected light do not arise.

ABOVE: Sundials are always a popular addition in the garden. This striking design has been used as the focal point in a garden room and will look handsome throughout the seasons.

PERGOLAS, ARCHES AND ARBOURS

An archway wreathed in a climbing rose at the entrance to an enclosed garden, or a series of archways over a path, create a feeling of intimacy and structure.

The Victorians, with their mania for decoration, introduced many pretty and distinctive styles. Arches are often constructed of wood and trellis which allow freedom of design, but limit their lifespan. Stone and brick archways are permanent and can be made to relate to many homes, but they can be expensive to construct.

A pergola serves several purposes. It can be employed to provide shelter on a garden wall, or it can be attached to a house creating a pleasant verandah. Used as a garden structure on which to grow grape vines, sweet briars, clematis, or wisteria, pergolas can be constructed in a variety of ways. At the end of the nineteenth century when the 'wild' garden was popular, they were often made of wood branches with the bark left on. Later designs were more architectural and were often constructed of stone, tile, or brick with heavy cross-beams.

An arbour as a central focal point to a geometric layout can be stunning, and is an elegant shape for roses and other climbers to grow over. Victorian wirework arbours, planted with roses such as 'Madame Alfred Carrière', are charming, and reproductions of these designs can be bought today. Iron arbours are also available or can be constructed.

SEATS

Because of the nature of the courtyard or patio garden with its enclosing boundaries, seating—like everything else—is on constant display and should be incorporated with great care. Locate seating so that it provides the user with a view, shelter, sun and comfort.

Providing a seat for people to enjoy the beauty of the area, or to have a meal, enables the area to be used as part of the home. The placement and choice of design should relate to the style of the garden and its layout.

The earliest type of seat recorded in European courtyards was the turf seat. Sometimes it was planted with a herb which would give off a fragrance when sat on. The problem with these seats was that they could only be used when the weather had been particularly dry for a long period.

Through the ages, craftsmen and artists have been called on to design and produce a variety of garden seats and tables. Reproductions of many of these designs are available today. However, quality, style and suitability govern choice. Simplicity is often the best answer if there is any doubt about style or colour.

LEFT: In this established garden room, a charming new rose arbour has been designed to provide a sheltered area to sit and enjoy the perfumes and colours of the garden. Complemented by the iron chair the arbour will soon be smothered in climbing roses and will become a pretty retreat and focal point of the garden layout.

ABOVE: *A once dreary brick wall has been successfully 'dressed' with a selection of containers and hanging baskets planted with* Begonias, Fuchsias, busy Lizzie *and ivy-leaved geraniums to brighten the whole area. With the container plants arranged at different heights to give added interest, and complemented with a small statue of a pretty girl, a potentially gloomy space has been made into a pleasant outdoor area. Designed by Christopher Masson.*

LEFT: *For sheer visual impact and fun, this exciting colour combination of blue seat, bright pink* Verbena x hybrida *planted in terracotta pots, and the stone and brick walling, would be hard to beat in a modern courtyard or patio garden. Sometimes a design deserves a real feast of colour — as has been added here — to give that special ingredient.*

ABOVE: In a garden where a large area of paving is required, care must be taken to choose a material which will complement the layout and the design of the total space. Changes of shape will often dictate the need to use a small-scale, regular design that can cope comfortably. The job of paving an area like this is best left to an expert, if such immaculate results are to be obtained. Designed by Barbara Wenzel.

PAVING

There are many paving materials to choose from. Hard surface paths can be made of brick, tile, natural stones or pebbles; flexible paths can be made of gravel, sand, ashes or shell, and soft paths of grass or creeping plants.

A courtyard or patio is generally designed to associate directly with the house and to provide an outside seating area for meals or play. Any decision about paving materials should be made with the finish of these elements in mind.

As with seating, simplicity in treatment, using one material rather than trying to incorporate a number in a small area, usually gives a superior result. If there are curved areas or steps leading to a change in level, choose a paving material that can cope with these conditions.

Bricks, stone and pebbles are attractive materials. Their small scale works well and they have a quality and timelessness about them, which makes them an excellent choice. Reconstituted stone products are readily available. Care must however be taken when choosing any of these to avoid uncomfortable shapes and unusual colours.

Gravel and shell paths work very well in some garden layouts. They need an edging to keep the material tidy and these days they are easy to keep weed-free with non-residual chemical sprays.

Quarry tiles and slate can be a successful surface in some circumstances. They have a tailored appearance and quality, which suits modern crisp design.

Soft paths planted with grass or creepers can be delightful if well maintained, but are not suitable in wet climates.

TOPIARY

Topiary—the trimming or training of trees or shrubs into decorative shapes—is an ancient art, which evolved from the Italian fashion of placing statues in garden designs. Geometrical topiary designs have always been popular and more ambitious projects have included a range of figures and shapes. The Victorians, with their love of eclectic and elaborate designs, were particularly keen on this gardening skill.

Seventeenth century Dutch courtyard gardens, which became a popular design in England in the late nineteenth century, were especially suitable for this art. They were small, enclosed by tall clipped hedges,and laid out in a formal geometric design with paved paths and simple flower beds outlined with box or lavender. At the axis of the paths a central or repeat pattern topiary design was often developed.

Common box is popular for small topiary and yews can be used for large specimens. Holly, Portuguese laurel and hemlock are also suitable. All topiary takes time and patience. It is however possible to speed up the process by planting several cuttings or bushes together at the one time. If cuttings are used, they need to come from the same clone so that they grow at a similar rate. In addition, all plants need to be fed regularly and well to encourage luxuriant growth.

Generally, with basic classic shapes, the plant or plants have to reach the desired height before being clipped or pruned into shape. Where the design is more complicated, it may be necessary to make a wire or cane frame to train the

ABOVE: The art of topiary can also be the art of adding a visual surprise, which has certainly been achieved with good humour and panache on this particular garden hedge.

plant as it grows. When a particular shape such as a sphere is wanted, but the plant grows in such a way that a pyramid would be more appropriate, it is usually better to follow nature's directions than to attempt to attain the impossible.

ESPALIER

Courtyards and patios offer the ideal environment in which to train small trees, shrubs and, in particular, fruit trees. Apples and pears, on extra dwarfing root-stocks, will normally not exceed 2m (6ft) in height, and are available from many stockists. Peaches and plums can also be successfully trained.

Regular pruning in both summer and winter encourages intensive crops, and because of the size and shape of espaliered trees and bushes, it is easy to spray and harvest them. The cordon is the simplest of all shapes, where the primary idea is to develop a single cord, rope or stem of leaves and fruit from a single root. An espalier-trained fruit tree consists of several tiers of horizontal branches growing from one vertical shoot.

There are excellent specialist books on this subject which are worth studying before beginning this type of gardening. Plant nurseries are also often happy to provide advice on a wide variety of plants which can be trained in this way.

MAINTAINING THE COURTYARD & PATIO

The Practicalities

Gardening can be fun, but all gardens require care and maintenance no matter what their style and size. Gardening involves bending, stretching, kneeling, climbing over and under things, and the clearing of rubbish after a maintenance session. To make life easier, wear clothes that are comfortable and can stand the odd snag or bit of dirt. Buy a pair of durable gardening gloves that fit well. Have a pair of shoes that can cope with being worn out of doors in all weathers. Finally, invest in good quality tools and equipment and look after them so that they can provide you with the maximum assistance.

LEFT: In a small garden everything is on display all the year around. Buying quality plants and paying attention to any special feeding and trimming requirements always pays dividends. This garden, with its small glasshouse for housing tender plants during winter and propagating new material, has been thoughtfully laid out and beautifully maintained. Designed by Richard Shelbourne.

PREVIOUS PAGE: A garden with an abundant planting scheme requires regular trimming and pruning to maintain its well-groomed presentation. Paths should be kept free of weeds, and overhanging foliage and the edges of the rectangle of grass neatly clipped. With a garden like this, it is desirable to have a service area, complete with compost bins, to make good use of the excess clippings.

The enclosed garden is a contained area which, because of its size and layout, is on display at all times. It therefore needs to be well maintained to ensure maximum visual pleasure.

TYPES OF SOILS

The texture and composition of the soil is of great importance. An ideal soil for growing plants of all kinds is a mixture of about 50 to 60 percent sand particles to about 30 percent clay, the rest being made up of partially decomposed organic material, or humus as it is commonly called. However, few people are lucky enough to have the perfect mix and must balance and feed the soil to help plant growth.

Clay soil is heavy and difficult to work. When wet, it becomes waterlogged and sticky, and when the sun shines it dries and cracks. To make it more fertile and easier to work, humus plus sand or grit should be added. The addition of lime can help break up the particles, although take care when adding it as a number of plants react unfavourably to this supplement.

Because sandy soil is composed of larger gritty particles, water tends to drain through it too quickly, taking vital nutrients with it. These soils can also be helped by the addition of humus.

Peat soils are composed of dead and decaying roots, rhizomes, stems and leaves. They are usually sour and require draining, liming and the addition of old or more fertile soil.

Volcanic soils vary in texture, but when mixed with humus can be very fertile.

If new raised planting beds are being created, often the most practical answer is to bring in new soil. Check the source of the supply very carefully. Ideally, the soil should be a good quality loam of medium texture, and free of weeds and chemicals.

FEEDING THE SOIL AND PLANTS

Creating a new planting scheme in an existing courtyard or patio garden often means that you remove most of the plants. This provides the opportunity to prepare the soil properly. Eradicating perennial weeds, such as bishop's weed or bindweed, is a tiresome but essential task which is well worth putting time and effort into. Solving this problem at the outset means you are not continually having to remove convolvulus from around your new and expensive plants.

Digging the soil and incorporating organic material in the form of animal manure or vegetable compost is one of the best ways of improving it.

Manure is made up in various ways, depending on the availability of materials. One of the best mixtures for a garden is horse manure and straw, but

ABOVE: Regular trimming and pruning is an essential task in this pretty garden. The climbing roses will respond well to the removal of dead or spindly growth, and an annual prune will encourage new growth and flower production. Mulching and feeding is also most important to ensure the healthy appearance of all the plants. Designed by Michael Balston.

this may not be readily obtainable. Check availability from the nursery or supplier.

Homemade garden compost formed from rotted vegetable waste is excellent. There are countless recipes available for successful combinations of material. Do not be put off from attempting to develop your own compost because of the time it takes to get a heap ready for incorporation into the garden. There are accelerants available that hasten the job.

Artificial fertilisers are used to supply essential food direct to plants. They help to stimulate plant growth, but do nothing to improve the physical properties of the soil. It is therefore very important to remember that fertilisers are not substitutes for manures or other organic materials that provide humus. The manufacturer's directions should be strictly adhered to when using and mixing these products.

MULCHING

Mulches are used to help improve plant growth by modifying soil temperature and reducing the evaporation of water. Mulching is also a valuable method of suppressing weed development.

Manure may be used for this purpose if it is in a well rotted condition. It will also perform the double task of enriching the ground. Leaf mould, partly-decayed leaves, some lawn cuttings, sawdust from untreated timber, and material from the compost heap will also work well. The mulch should be sufficiently open to allow the passage of water to the soil and the even circulation of air to assist in the decomposition of the leaf material.

It is most important to provide mulch around newly planted trees and shrubs, particularly those planted in spring. It should be spread to a depth of 10–12cm (4–5in) as far as the roots extend, but should not be piled up around the base of the trunk.

In easy-care gardens, woodchip mulches have become popular. They need to be spread with care and in a sufficient quantity to get a good even coverage. Regular maintenance is also necessary to avoid untidy bare patches which allow extra weeds to develop. Plastic sheeting under wood chips should be used with caution. The plastic can heat up in summer and cook the roots of plants.

TRIMMING AND PRUNING

During her long gardening career, Vita Sackville-West gave much good advice to gardeners. On the subject of pruning, she suggested that although it may be a terrifying thing to cut into living wood, we should never hesitate to chop away dead rubbish which nature herself has discarded. She also said that any clutter of twigs should be removed, especially in the centre of a shrub, to let in the light and air.

In essence, the main reasons to undertake serious trimming and pruning are to remove dead and straggly wood, to cut down large overgrown plants, to encourage new and vigorous flowering stems on shrubs that flower on last year's wood, to restrict the size of shrubs that flower only on new wood, to clear out old wood, and to restrict the size of climbing plants. Pruning should be done when a plant has reached its yearly period of minimum growth, usually in winter. Prune with an eye to the plant's natural shape.

WEEDING

Controlling weeds can be assisted by understanding what you are dealing with, and by regular hoeing and mulching.

There are two types of weeds, annuals and perennials. Annuals appear in the spring and summer. They grow rapidly, flower, seed profusely, and then die off. Perennials are more difficult to deal with. They possess a twitch (which is an underground creeping system), a bulbous habit, or an extremely vigorous tap root.

To control annual weeds, use a sharp hoe regularly to prevent them flowering and setting seed. Weeds that are cut off just below the soil surface are readily killed. If the weather is hot, the plant will die in a day or two with exposure to the sun. However, in cooler weather, it may be necessary to rake up the weeds and remove them completely.

With perennials, carefully remove any plants that appear. This must include not just what you can see on the surface of the ground, but also everything underneath it. Burn all refuse or ensure that it is disposed of satisfactorily.

Chemical weed eradication should only be used as a last resort. Garden plants are very susceptible to chemical poisons and it is too easy to lose valuable plants with this method of control.

PREVENTING PESTS AND DISEASES

The incidence of pests and diseases can be minimised by correct cultivation and rigid weed control. Affected plants can generally be treated quickly and successfully with one of the many forms of insecticides and treatments available. Look for environmentally friendly products and always follow the manufacturer's directions carefully. Take special care to store products in a safe place.

Several factors govern the health of plant life. Two of the most important are feeding and watering. A satisfactory soil should contain sufficient nourishment, as poorly fed plants are very susceptible to disease. Conversely, too much manure or fertiliser will cause rank and weak growth. Watering is also essential and should be done at regular intervals to keep roots moist.

Keeping a vigilant eye on your garden will help spot unhealthy, or discoloured plants. Identify the problem as soon as possible, and take remedial action.

Some pests can be discouraged by the use of companion planting, which is a concept introduced in the 1900s by Dr Rudolf Steiner. Certain types of herbs and flowers are considered to be particularly useful for this purpose. Catnip (*Nepeta cataria*), for example, contains an insect repellant oil; nasturtium (*Tropaeolum*) repels borer from fruit trees; and flowering onion (*Allium*) planted with roses will protect them from aphids. There are countless other examples well worth investigating if you are particularly interested in organic control.

In addition to the use of plants as natural deterrents, many pests can be controlled by encouraging their natural predators. Ladybirds (ladybugs) feed on aphids, scale insects and the eggs and larvae of other small insects; lacewings eat thrips, mites, caterpillar eggs, scales, aphids and mealy bugs; and the praying mantis also devours aphids.

CONTAINER GARDENING

A brief history

Containers are versatile, fashionable, adaptive and responsive, and can provide a touch of colour or an elegant sophisticated accent in any room or garden.

Urns, sinks, shoes, old pots and pottery vases are just some of the items put to use as containers for growing flowers, vegetables, herbs, fruits and ferns.

Containers have appeared in homes, gardens, parks and patios throughout history. The Greeks used them to adorn their classical temples, the Romans to supply colour in their peristyle gardens, the Italians to dress the terraces of their magnificent country retreats, and the French to grow fruit trees in to adorn the stately grounds of their chateaux.

In England, containers were always a special feature of a garden room, and were cleverly used as a focal point in a formal design or to dress up a niche or to top a wall. In the New World they were added to gardens of all styles.

In the Victorian era, a front parlour would have been considered incomplete without its potted table palm

LEFT: Spring is announced with this cheerful display of daffodils planted in containers and in the garden beds. The handrail has been cleverly positioned on the entrance steps to allow space for a row of containers to be placed in safety away from passing traffic. In large containers, plant bulbs in two or three layers for an extended flowering season and for a better display.

ABOVE: At Tintinhull House in Somerset, England, simple containers with an informal planting scheme of white Marguerite daisies and Diascia are used near the house to add seasonal colour.

PREVIOUS PAGE: In this small outdoor garden room, a beautiful container garden has been created to enliven the mellow tones of the paving and brick walls that clad the house. Half barrels and hanging baskets have been 'landscaped' with roses, Fuchsia, Lobelia, ivy leaved geraniums and Nicotiana. The choice of plants and style of planting suit the location perfectly, and will provide enjoyment when viewed from outside or through the windows of the house. Designed by Bill Moran.

(*Aspidistra*), the butt of many music hall jokes. And in the 1960s, no self-respecting student flat or apartment would have been complete without its struggling rubber plant (*Ficus elastica*) in the corner.

Vita Sackville-West, the creator of the Sissinghurst garden, was known to bemoan the lack of imagination of the English in their use of containers, but was quick to point out the charm of the European enclosed garden bedecked with pots, or the flight of stairs brightened with a row of colourful containers.

Landscaping with container plants

Container gardening has grown in popularity, as people find both their time limited and their gardening space restricted. The art has come of age, with new soil mixes, slow release fertilisers, water retentive additives, and a whole host of miniature plants to adorn pots and other containers.

Containers can be used as a window garden or to brighten a front door. They can be hung at different levels to add interest to a blank wall, or placed as decoration on a patio or around a pool. Inside the home they add a special quality to rooms and sun porches. In the summerhouse they can be used to create a special effect with seasonal planting, and in the conservatory they are used to grow tender plants from exotic locations. Their use is never ending. It is just a matter of using your imagination and developing an eye for the right place and for the right type of container.

The location for pots is generally determined by the aesthetic qualities the addition of a container or group of containers will bring to an environment. Having decided on a location, the important questions are: what area is to be filled? how much money can be invested? what plant types will tolerate the amount of sun or shade they are to be put into? and how much time is available to care for the new additions to the home?

Like all planting schemes, scale is an important aspect. Before buying anything, take a careful look at the site and make a realistic assessment of the amount of material that will be required to make an effective display. The problem is usually not that something is too large for the area, but that the containers are too small to have sufficient impact. If this is the case, the solution may be to have a row of containers or a group of pots sitting at different heights. Alternatively, it may be possible to fill one very large container with several small pots to create the right effect.

Position is important too. A container should be placed where it will not be knocked over. If it is to be at head height near an entranceway, there must be sufficient room for people to be able to pass by comfortably, even when the plants are fully grown. Wind can do tremendous damage and plants can either be battered to death in a wind tunnel or otherwise suffer because the soil dries out too quickly. If a container is raised on a pedestal or bench, make sure the wind cannot send it flying in a storm.

If a terrace or a balcony or a rooftop are to be the site of the container garden, two other important points need to be considered: weight and water.

It is surprising how much a full container of wet soil can weigh. Once a group of them are put together in one area, the total load can be too much for some structures. Planting in lightweight containers using light artificial soil can help. Where a group of pots is to be used, check to see whether a supporting beam or post is close to the location, and make use of this additional support. Also consider spreading the load by placing the containers in a row or in some other interesting arrangement.

Watering the contents of containers is a practical problem wherever they are located and must be thought out carefully. If the garden is on a roof or balcony, special care is required. First, see if water is available on the roof or near the balcony. If it is not, carrying water from a distance may be the only answer unless a hose can be connected from further away. Check to see where excess water will run off. Many balconies are sloped so that rain water will drain off naturally. However, if the drainage of excess water affects neighbours below, this is a problem that will have to be dealt with.

LEFT: A delightfully stylish scene has been created in this London garden with the clever juxtaposition of plants and containers. An urn is surrounded by the mid-green fleshy leaves of a Hosta sieboldiana 'Elegans', *a topiary of box* (Buxus sempervirens), *and in the foreground three charming painted pots with bright blue and white stripes. Designed by Anthony Noel.*

A *planting scheme for a container garden*

Containers offer the opportunity to plant a garden with a variety of species which demand different soil conditions, feeding requirements and weather preferences. This design, which would work equally well in a small backyard or as a rooftop garden, includes varieties to suit both shady and sunny areas; it also provides an area for storage and work.

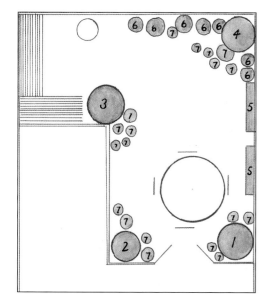

Key to planting sheme

1 *Albizia julibrissen*
2 *Laurus nobilis* (standard)
3 *Ailanthus altissima*
4 *Robinia pseudoacacia*
5 *Trachelospermum jasminoides*
6 Permanent shrubs:
      Ilex aquifolium (cone)
      Camellia japonica
      Viburnum tinus (ball)
      Buxus sempervirens (ball)
      Azaleas
      Ferns
7 Bulbs, perennials, annuals, herbs

Many different sizes and shapes of terracotta pots, lightly whitewashed, have been used to plant this container garden. The space is an area typical of those found at the rear of a town house or on the roof of an apartment block. It is divided into three distinct areas: shady, sunny and work.

The planting scheme is a mix of formal and informal shapes allowing ample scope for seasonal changes. In the working area a potting bench is located. Underneath it there is room for storing composts, fertilisers and spare pots. A tap (spigot) is located at one end of the potting bench. To assist with watering hanging baskets and dunking other containers, a half barrel (which would normally be kept full of water) has been sunk into the paving.

Trees have been planted in the largest pots to break the lines of the corners. The silk tree (*Albizia julibrissen*) by the house will form a dainty canopy, while the *Robinia pseudoacacia*, with its fine lime-green canopy, will make a striking contrast to the group of topiary shrubs and annuals at its feet. Near the house in the sunniest corner, some herbs have been included amongst the perennials and annuals.

A special background has been created for the dining area with the two terracotta troughs planted with star jasmine (*Trachelospermum jasminoides*). This charming evergreen plant produces masses of fragrant white flowers and has been clipped on to some trellis panels.

Gardening in containers

Planting schemes for containers have now become as interesting as those for conventional garden beds. Whereas the emphasis was initially on one plant to a pot, it is now on landscaping a container. Gardens in containers are treated like flower arrangements. They are designed with contrasting or compatible colours in mind. Thought therefore needs to be given to the mix of leaf forms and textures. They also need to have a focal point, foreground planting and, in some instances, seasonal effects to complete a scheme.

ABOVE: Containers come in all shapes and sizes. In this back garden, a simple handcart has been constructed and filled with Lobelia and Pelargonium to create a pretty summer display. Pink yarrow in the background complements the picture.

LEFT: At Bourton House in Gloucester, England, terracotta pots in a variety of sizes have been grouped together to provide a display of Begonia, Pelargonium, a Triphylla Fuchsia and the Dahlia 'Bishop of Llandaf'. The predominantly rich red colour tones contrast well against the mellow stone.

SOME MIXED PLANTING SCHEMES FOR CONTAINERS

A white and grey container
Cosmos White, tall
Nicotiana White
Senecio 'Silver Dust'
Omphalodes linifolia
Lobelia White
Zinnia 'Envy'

A blue, purple and lemon scheme
Centaurea (cornflower) Blue, tall
Scabiosa atropurpurea
Cheiranthus Lemon
Anemone 'de Caen' Single, blue
Ageratum Dwarf, blue
Pansies Lemon

Sunset colours, blue and purple
Salpiglossis sinuata Yellow and bronze
Cheiranthus Golds and browns
Petunias Yellow
Salvia horminum (Clary sage) Purple
Nigella damascena Soft blue
Pansies Soft blue

A pink and grey container
Cosmos 'Sensation' Bright pink
Helichrysum petiolare
Bellis perennis
Pelargonium peltatum (ivy geranium) Pink
Silene (*Viscaria*) Bright pink
Schizanthus Pink
Senecio 'Silver Dust'

ABOVE: In the corner of this garden room a half barrel has been used to plant a standard rose in a sea of thyme foliage. Roses can be grown in containers successfully provided they have room for their roots to develop and the soil is fertile and well drained. Place roses in a position where they get plenty of sun and are protected from strong wind. Designed by Marion Smith.

Although trees and shrubs can be grown successfully in pots for years, it is important in the first instance not to over-pot them. Choose a container that is a comfortable size for the root ball. As the plant grows it should be re-potted. This should be undertaken each spring or autumn after the second year. Remove the plant and replant it in a container that will provide a couple of inches or so of extra room all around. Alternatively, a plant can be root pruned. To do this, remove the plant from its container when it is dormant and dry. Cut away matted roots and old compost and then re-pot it into the container with fresh crocks and new compost worked in well around the roots.

To get the most out of a flowering or fruiting shrub, the roots should fill a container by mid-summer. This ensures that the plant's energy goes into producing flowers or fruit rather than more roots.

Bedding plants and perennials should be packed into a container to give the best display. Deadheading will encourage these plants to flower all summer long, as this prevents them from forming seed. If seeds are required, delay seed production until towards the end of the season. After gathering the seeds, store them in a cool dry situation until they are needed for sowing next spring.

Bulbs for spring can be planted in two or three layers in a container to spread out their flowering time. Alternatively, a selection of early and late flowering species or cultivars will achieve the same result.

Edible crops are also popular container plants whether they are grown on their own, or mixed together with herbs and flowers for a more interesting display. Crops that can be grown this way include eggplants, cucumbers, various lettuces, snow peas, welsh leeks and tomatoes.

Herbs grown on the window ledge or by the back door are a family tradition. The choice of herbs tends to be very personal, as different types suit different styles of cooking. Some of the most versatile and popular herbs to grow are sweet and spicy globe basil, chives, coriander, garlic, mint, parsley, tarragon and thyme.

Fruiting trees can look spectacular and be very successfully grown in containers. However, standard varieties are not suitable as they soon become too big. Look for apples, pears, peaches and nectarines on dwarf root-stock for good results. Figs and persimmons are also interesting plants to grow in containers. Avoid plums or apricots unless there are sufficient plants to ensure pollination.

Citrus trees look beautiful in containers and grow well. Sweet cumquat or japonica are very popular too. Cultivars of oranges, grapefruit, limes and lemons are also good species. In areas with cold winters, it is necessary to take these plants inside during this season, or at least to protect their pots with some kind of insulation.

RIGHT: A group of smaller sized terracotta pots has been used to complement the beautifully tailored planting boxes specifically constructed for this city garden. Filled with flowering and trailing plants, the different scale and shape of the containers helps to soften the overall effect and adds variety to the garden. Designed by Tim du Val.

Choosing a container

Anything and everything has been and can be used as a container in which to grow plants. As long as it can hold enough potting mix, has adequate drainage, and is sympathetic to the plant material and its surroundings, it will make a good container.

Antique terracotta, urns, cast iron and stone containers are all available at a price. Reconstituted stone, concrete, and simple rot-resistant wooden containers are all readily available from a wide variety of sources. Choose the container according to the position it is to occupy, the size and number needed, and the materials that will surround it.

Natural materials like stone and terracotta have always been popular, and look particularly good against brick, tile and other traditional building materials. Reconstituted stone, fibreglass and plastic tend to be more suitable for use with modern building materials.

Containers can look very attractive grouped together. Place those containing large trees and shrubs at the back, with containers of annuals and perennials

LEFT: Growing a variety of herbs and flowers together, close to the kitchen door, can provide a visual treat as well as some lovely additions to the menu. A group of terracotta pots has been used here to grow lilies (Lilium Regale), Nicotiana, rosemary, and a mix of herbs and summer flowers. Designed by Sue Berger.

filling the front spaces. If a planting scheme is large and requires a number of containers, and if the mature plants spread and cascade over the sides of pots, it is possible to make use of less attractive containers in the background where they will be hidden, and place a few special ones at the front.

TERRACOTTA

Terracotta pots are beautiful and timeless. They have appeared throughout history in simple shapes or heavily adorned with swags and mythical beasts. Sizes range from enormous to tiny and suit every type of planting material.

Plants grow well in terracotta, as plant roots can breath through their porous walls. In summer, the root ball remains relatively cool, and in winter the pot provides a reasonable degree of insulation.

Rough handling can, however, easily cause chipping and flaking, and as terracotta contains moisture it is susceptible to frost damage. Buy containers that come with a guarantee against frost damage, if you live in a frost-prone area.

In time, terracotta develops a charming patina. It is possible to speed up this process in a number of ways. The most natural way is to stand the pot in wet grass or under dripping trees or a leaking gutter so that moss can develop.

Alternatively, a pot left standing in bright sunshine will soon develop grey-white patches. In addition, a pot can be painted with liquid fertiliser or brushed with water in which comfrey leaves or manure has been soaked. Live yoghurt or sour milk will also help with artificial 'aging'. If a lighter colour is desired, a wash of lime is very attractive; or a light coat of thin water based paint will alter the colour completely.

GLAZED EARTHENWARE

A wide range of decorative glazed ceramic pots is available on the market. These can make delightful containers and are the ideal pot if a totally colour co-ordinated scheme is planned. Glazing is, however, very susceptible to frost damage and cracks extremely easily. Again, look for the pots that have a manufacturer's guarantee against this problem.

CONCRETE AND RECONSTITUTED STONE

There are some excellent containers available in concrete and reconstituted stone materials. They range from replicas of traditional urns and vases to smooth symmetrical creations, and are very durable and versatile. Buy only quality products and avoid the very crudely cast pieces on the market.

FIBREGLASS AND FIBREGLASS/ CONCRETE CONTAINERS

A blend of fibreglass and concrete produces a thin-walled container which is as durable as concrete. The material has a smooth finish, and because it is lighter than concrete, containers made of this product can be useful in a variety of situations.

Fibreglass containers are even lighter in weight and are reasonably durable. Ideally they should be used in indoor situations, but can also be used in sheltered positions. As they tend to look very shiny and modern, they should be restricted to suitably sympathetic surroundings.

PLASTIC

Plastic is a love/hate material for planting pots. On the plus side, it is inexpensive and lightweight and the pots come in a range of colours and sizes to match every type of situation and plant. The heavier more flexible pots last reasonably well. In contrast, the thin rigid pots tend to break easily and their shiny finish can detract from many situations. However, by containing plants that grow to cover most of the pot, they can work well.

WOODEN CONTAINERS

Wood is a very good insulating material and because it is natural, suits a variety of situations. Wooden containers can be built or bought in many shapes and sizes. Ideally, always use naturally rot-resistant timbers such as cedar or California redwood. Cheaper wooden containers are usually made from pine and are treated to withstand moisture problems. They normally do not last as long as the others.

HANGING BASKETS

Hanging baskets come in various sizes in wire and plastic. They are lightweight, which is important, because once they are filled with a liner, potting mixture and plants, and are watered, they can become extremely heavy. Wall baskets are also widely available and are made in wire as well as terracotta and ceramic. Place hanging containers where people will not knock into them and where they are not affected by the wind. Brackets to secure the container to the wall are usually sold with the container. Always check that they are adequate to support the weight of the basket and are securely fastened.

RIGHT: Petunias (Petunia) are very popular flowers for both the garden and container growing. They flower over a long period, tolerate very hot days provided they are adequately watered, are produced in a variety of colours, and can easily be grown from seed. Here they stand apart from the cheerful surrounding flower beds in their very own special log container.

FOLLOWING PAGE: An unusual combination of colours and textures works well in this window box designed to brighten an autumn day. The delicate sprays of ivy (Hedera helix) are counter-balanced with a mix of heaths and heathers, yellow chrysanthemums and Jerusalem cherries. Designed by Susie Ind, Pimlico Flowers.

PLANTS FOR CONTAINERS

Choosing plants

Before choosing any plants to grow in a container, ask a local nursery or garden centre whether they are suitable for your particular climatic conditions.

TREES

Fruiting

Ficus carica (fig)
Malus pumila (apple) (dwarf root-stock)
Pyrus communis (pear) (dwarf root-stock)
Prunus persica (peach) (dwarf root-stock)
Prunus persica cv (nectarine) (dwarf root-stock)
Diospyros (persimmon)

For large containers:
Key
AC   Autumn colour
D   Deciduous
E   Evergreen

Acer palmatum (Japanese maple) D AC All varieties, good foliage and habit
Ailanthus altissima (tree of heaven) D Elegant leaves
Albizzia julibrissen (silk tree) D Dainty canopy

Arbutus unedo (strawberry tree) E White flowers, red fruit
Azara microphylla E Dainty weeping foliage
Elaeagnus angustifolia E Silver foliage, creamy yellow flowers
Eucalyptus spp, incl *E. cinerea* E Varied, aromatic foliage
Fraxinus oxycarpa 'Raywood' (claret ash) D AC Good foliage
    ornus D Creamy white flowers, summer
Gleditsia triacanthos (honey locust) D Elegant foliage
Ilex aquifolium (holly) E Bold foliage, red berries
Laurus nobilis (bay tree) E Attractive aromatic foliage
Malus (crab apple) D All varieties, attractive spring flowers, autumn fruit
Prunus lusitanicus (Portugese laurel) E Good foliage, white flowers
Rhus typhina 'Laciniata' D AC Bold cut leaves
Robinia pseudoacacia D Fine foliage, good habit
Sorbus aria (whitebeam) D AC Simple, toothed leaves, crimson fruit
    aucuparia (rowan) D AC Pinnate leaves, bright red fruit
Quercus ilex (holm oak) E Grey-green foliage

ANNUALS

Anemone 'de Caen' Red, white or blue poppies, spring
Ageratum houstonianum (blue floss flower) Various varieties
Aurinia maritima White fragrant flowers on mats
Bellis perennis (daisy) Large flower, pink, white, red
Brassica cleracea (kale) Pink or white coloured leaves
Cheiranthus cheiri (wallflowers) Dense spike, yellow, red, purple
Centaurea (cornflower) Pretty, tall flowers
Cosmos 'Sensation' Daisy flowers, summer, finely cut leaves
Dorotheanthus bellidiformis (Livingstone daisies) Daisies on mats
Helichrysum petiolare Silvery-grey leaved trailer
Impatiens walleriana (busy Lizzie) White through pink to purple and scarlet flowers
Lobelia erinus (blue mats) Hardy mats of flowers
Nemesia strumosa Multicoloured small plants
Nicotiana, dwarf Pink, white and red flowers perfumed at night
Nigella damascena (Love-in-a-mist) Filigree foliage, cornflower blue flowers

Omphalodes linifolia Compact habit, pretty leaf
Pansy Pretty flowers, good low edging plant
Petunia Often trailing stems, large trumpet flowers
Pelargonium peltatum (ivy geranium) Masses of showy flowers
Phlox drummondii Multicoloured, low growing
Polyanthus Spring flowering, many colours
Primula malacoides Carmine rose flowers
Salpiglossis sinuata Beautifully marked flowers, yellows, browns
Salvia horminium (Clary sage) Compact bush, pink, blue
Scabiosa atropurpurea Purple flowers, summer
Schizanthus pinnatus (poor man's orchid) Dainty stems
Senecio maritima Lobed leaves silvery appearance
Silene (*Viscaria*) Small pink flowers
Tagetes patula and *T. erecta* (marigolds) Yellow, orange flowers
Viola Low edging plant
Zinnia elegans Stiff blooms, good for picking
    'Envy' Green flowers, good for cutting

SHRUBS

Aucuba japonica E Bold leaves, red berries
Azalea Choose evergreen varieties. Spectacular spring blossom
Buxus sempervirens (English box) E Tolerates dense shade
Camellia japonica E Good foliage, pink or red flowers, winter, spring
    x Williamsii E Good foliage, pink or red flowers
Chrysanthemum frutescens (marguerite daisy) Flowers over long period
Fuchsia hybrids D Hanging flowers, summer
Heliotropium peruvianum E Perfumed heliotrope flowers, summer
Hydrangea macrophylla (dwarf) D Big summer heads
Plumbago auriculata E Sky-blue flowers, summer
Rhododendron E Good foliage, large flowers, spring
Trachelospermum jasminoides (star jasmine) E Masses of fragrant
white flowers
Viburnum tinus E Good foliage, pink flowers

For a more tropical look:
Bamboos Attractive stems and clump-forming habit, dainty foliage
    Phyllostachys bambusoides
                flexuosa
                        viridiglaucescens
    Pseudosasa japonica
    Sasa veitchii
    Semiarundinaria fastuosa
Cordyline australis (NZ cabbage tree) E Bold strap-like leaves
Fatsia japonica E Shiny bold leaves for shade
Phormium tenax E Sword-like leaves
Trachycarpus fortunei (Chinese fan palm) E Hardy
Yucca E Sword-like leaves

PERENNIALS

Agapanthus praecox Strap-shaped leaves, striking flowers
Astilbe x arendsii Plumy spires over attractively cut leaves
Bergenia cordifolia Big glossy evergreen leaves
Clivia miniata Orange-scarlet funnel-shaped flowers
Francoa ramosa (may) Plumes, small white flowers
Hedera helix (ivy) Leaves of various forms and colours
Helleborus niger Large waxy pink or white flowers
Helichrysum petiolare Low growing grey-green foliage

Hemerocallis (day lily) Variety of colours, grass-like foliage
Hosta Fragrant lily-like flowers
Kniphofia hybrids (red hot poker) Orange-red spikes of tubular flowers
Liriope muscari (turf lily) Purple flowers, autumn
Pelargonium peltatum (geranium) Wide colour range, shrubby
Soleirolia soleirolii (as a ground cover) Forms attractive carpet
Verbena varieties Rich colours, fragrant blooms

FERNS

These ferns have dainty foliage and enjoy damp, shady conditions.

Athyrium filix-femina
Asplenium trichomanes
Blechnum capense
Dryopteris corusca
        erythrosora
        squamaestipes
        filix-mas
        varia

Onoclea sensibilis
Phyllitis scolopendrium
Polypodium vulgare
                glycyrrhiza
Polystichum aculeatum
                setiferum
                angulare

HERBS

Basil, sweet and spicy globe
Chervil
Chives
Coriander
Cress
Dill
Garlic

Marjoram
Mint
Parsley
Rosemary
Sage
Summer Savory
Tarragon
Thyme

BULBS

Amaryllis belladonna (naked ladies) Tall perfumed pink, white flowers, autumn
Anemone coronaria 'De Caen' Like small poppies, good cut flowers
Begonia (tuberous) Exotic large blooms in many colours
Daffodil Especially tazettas and poetaz forms, which are tender
    Beersheba Pure white
    Carbineer Yellow and orange
    Carlton Pale yellow
    Charity May Small canary yellow
    Chérie Small white and pink
    Cragford Clusters of white and orange
    Cheerfulness Double white clusters
    February Gold Small yellow trumpets
    Foresight Yellow and white
    Grand Emperor White and orange clusters
    Grand Monarch White and lemon clusters
    Gloriosus White and orange clusters
    Geranium Clusters of white and orange-red flowers
    Golden Harvest Large golden yellow
    Jenny Small white and primrose yellow
    John Evelyn Large white and apricot orange
    King Alfred Large golden yellow
    Paperwhite Clusters of early white flowers
    Scarlet Elegance Yellow and orange
    Silver Chimes Small white and lemon clusters
    Soleil d'Or Yellow and orange clusters
    Scarlet Gem Small yellow and orange red
    St. Agnes White and orange red
    Tête-à-Tête Small yellow
    Thalia Clusters of pure white
    Trevithian Clusters of rich yellow

    Van Sion Double yellow
    Yellow Cheerfulness Double yellow clusters
Freesia Often fragrant, good for cutting
Hyacinth Fragrant stems
Iris Dutch and Spanish Tall stems good for cutting. Blue, white, yellow flowers
    laevigata (Japanese iris) Light to deep-violet flower
Lilies:
Lilium bakerinum Creamy white
    brownii White and brown
    concolor Scarlet
    formosanum Pure white, scented
    hansonii Yellow orange
    x hollandicum Oranges and yellows
    japonicum Pale pink
    x maculatum Yellow-orange-red
    nobilissimum White
    primulinum Greenish yellow
    pumilum Scarlet
    regale White, yellow throat
    rubellum Rosy pink
    sulphureum Yellow and white
    speciosum Pink, white
Muscari (grape hyacinth) Blue spring flowers
Nerine Tall pink lily-like flowers, autumn
Ranunculus asiaticus (florists ranunculus) Good for cutting
Sprekelia (Jacobite lily) Elegant red lily-like flowers
Tulipa (tulip) Epecially early flowering singles and doubles, the Duc van Tol varieties and other smaller species
Zantedeschia (Arum lily) Yellow or white flowers good for cutting

VEGETABLES

Aubergine (eggplant)
Courgette (zucchini)
Cucumber
Dwarf beans
Lettuce, smaller kinds
Peas, esp. snow peas
Peppers

Potatoes (new)
Radish
Shallots
Silverbeet and Ruby Chard
Spring onions
Tomatoes
Welsh leeks

RIGHT: A glorious display of tulips (Tulipa) has been grown in half barrels which sit comfortably under mature trees. Tulips come in a wide variety of colours and sizes and require a sunny, sheltered position.

CONTAINER MAINTENANCE

The Practicalities

Containers can be messy to work with so it is advisable to have an appropriate area available for the chores. Potting mix can easily be spilled on the floor when containers are being filled, and the occasional overflow when watering must be expected. An adequate permanent storage area for soils, fertilisers and equipment is also essential.

POTTING MIXTURES

Getting the soil mix right for container-grown plants is as important as it is for other gardens. Because of the confined space in which the plant or plants are going to grow, the soil must contain the

LEFT: Screens of trellis work and a Versailles-style box painted a rich green have been chosen to decorate a once blank wall. The hydrangea (Hydrangea paniculata) is a pretty choice as its delicate flower heads contrast with the rich colour tones of the container and background wall.

PREVIOUS PAGE: An assortment of containers has been successfully used in the corner of this London garden. The terracotta pots and the urn mounted on its pedestal and planted with a variegated Agave add a dramatic note to the combination.

right proportion of essential plant foods such as nitrogen, potash and phosphate. In addition, the mix must be free of pests and diseases.

When you are buying plants to grow in containers, check with the nursery whether there are any special instructions for particular species. Nurseries normally sell a range of potting mixes, which consist of loam, peat and sand with varying proportions of fertiliser. Some will have a choice of both peat and soil-based potting mixes. The peat base will dry out quickly if it is not watered on a regular basis. In contrast, some soil-based mixes can become compacted and heavy. A combination of the two is often the ideal combination.

In general, a lightly fertilised potting compost should be used for seedlings and young plants. For more mature specimens use a mix that has a higher proportion of fertiliser.

PLANTING

If you are using a new container, rinse it out first with water and dry it carefully to remove any manufacturing residues. If the container is an old one, make sure it is completely clean and free of old soil.

Scrub the inside with a weak solution of bleach or disinfectant to eliminate diseased organisms.

Porous containers, such as terracotta or stone, need special attention. They can soak up moisture from the potting mix and deprive a newly planted specimen of its essential food supply. For this reason, it is very important to soak these types of containers well and air-dry them before use.

Choose a container that is going to hold whatever you plant in it comfortably with enough space around the root syst em. Place some pieces of clean drainage material, such as broken pieces of terracotta, small stones or pieces of polystyrene, at the base of the container, and then put a layer of potting mix over it.

Next, place the plant in position so that the top of the root system is about 2.5cm (1in) below the top of the pot when it is covered with soil. Hold the plant steady and add more mix around the sides and over the top of the root system. Fill the pot to the top and then gently tap the pot on a hard surface to settle the potting mix. Top it up if necessary, firm the plant in lightly, and finally water thoroughly.

REPOTTING

A sure sign that a plant needs repotting is the sight of roots growing out of the holes in the base of the container. In general, after the second year, young plants need to be repotted each year in spring or early autumn.

Soak the plant before trying to remove it from the container. Next, gently hold the stem of the plant between your fingers and cover as much of the soil as you can by spreading out your hand. Turn the pot upside down and tap it on the bottom to loosen the ball of soil. The roots, which will probably have started to grow in a spiral, will need to be handled carefully. When you have removed the plant from the container, loosen the roots gently to encourage downward and sideways growth, and repot in a larger container.

WATERING

Aim to keep container-grown plants in a 'just moist' state. More plants are killed by overwatering and becoming water-logged, or by drying out, than by any other means.

Although plants generally need more water in the growing and flowering periods of late spring and summer than in the resting periods of autumn or winter, it is important to check for moisture frequently. This is in part because the leaf area of a potted plant will often shelter the soil of the pot it is in, and make it difficult for rainwater to penetrate through to the root system. Avoid watering when the weather is icy because the water could freeze in the pot.

Give plants a good watering at least once a week in warm weather and once every two weeks in the winter. Do not leave them sitting in a dish of water as this may result in root rot.

FEEDING

Individual plants have different feeding requirements, so seek advice on what is needed when you acquire a new one.

As a general rule, apply liquid fertiliser once a week especially during the growing season. There are various products on the market to select from. Follow the manufacturer's directions carefully.

HOLIDAY TIME

Plants that are left unattended for a period, particularly in the summer, will need extra attention. Move containers out of the direct sunlight and into the shade. To help reduce the amount of water that will be required, remove flowers and buds by cutting them off cleanly.

There are several automatic watering systems available which might be worth investing in if you go away frequently. Alternatively, set up a homemade capillary watering system. This can be done quite simply with the aid of a bucket of water and a length of paraffin lamp wick. Cut lengths of wick to reach from the bottom of the bucket of water into the soil of each planted container. Wet the wick and the water will seep through into the pots for an extended period.

Plants can also be kept moist for several days by packing them into a box and surrounding them with damp peat or newspaper packed firmly around the pots. Place them in a shady position.

If, after all your efforts, you come home to find a precious plant wilted and to all intents and purposes dead, try the following. Scrape the main stem fairly low down, but above the lowest branching side shoot. If it shows green there is still some life left in the plant.

Lift the entire plant out of its container. Trim the roots back to firm shoots showing green when they are cut. Repot the plant in a new potting mix, but do not add any fertilisers or tonics. Next, soak the pot and plant in a bucket of water until bubbles stop rising. Drain and place in light but not bright sunlight. Let the potting mix get fairly dry, then soak the whole pot again.

PESTS AND DISEASES

To avoid pests and diseases, start off with plants potted in clean containers using new potting mix. Reusing potting mix can cause more problems than it is worth. Place pots in clean dry areas when they are not in use. Leaves and weeds can provide the ideal home for slugs and mites.

Lack of healthy vigorous growth and poor foliage is often the result of incorrect watering, too much or too little feed, or the plant being root bound. Check these factors first.

If the problem is the result of a pest attack or disease, identify the cause and treat it as soon as possible. There are products on the market for every possible type of disease and pest. However, try organically-based products or simple organic solutions such as soapy water (but not detergents) for aphids as the first line of attack.

Index

Acknowledgements

A special thank you to my husband Derek for his assistance and encouragement, to my son Nicholas for his patience and to Martin Keay, who provided the planting details which I am sure will inspire many.

PHOTOGRAPHY CREDITS

Eric Crichton p.4, p.55

Robert Estall p.91

Garden and Landscape Pictures *Back cover* (Crawley Down Garden, Mrs Hudson), *p.79* (Lothian Garden, Mr and Mrs Reid), *p.81* (Greenwich Garden, Macartney House, Mrs & Mrs Wilson)

Gil Hanly *p.84*

Jerry Harpur *pp.2/3* (Lower Hall, Worfield), *p.6* (Designer: Ann Alexander-Sinclair), *p.8* (Helen Preston, Chelsea), *p.9* (Villandry), *p.11* (The Cloisters, New York), *pp.13* (Sissinghurst), *p.16* (Designer: Thomas Church, San Francisco), *pp.18/19* (Ann Griot, Los Angeles), *p.20* (Designer: Keyes Landscape, Camden), *pp.29* (Designer: Michael Balston), *p.32* (Designer: Tim du Val, New York), *pp.37* (Lower Hall, Worfield), *pp.58/59, p.60* (Designer: Susan Whittington), *p.63, p.66, p.69, p.72, p.78* (Designer: Gail Jenkins, Melbourne, Vic.), *p.89* (Designer: Christopher Masson), *p.90* (Designer: Barbara Wenzel, Melbourne, Vic.), *pp.92/93, p.94* (Designer: Richard Shelbourne), *p.96* (Designer: Michael Balston), *pp.98/99* (Designer: Bill Moran), *p.108* (Designer: Marion Smith), *p.109* (Designer: Tim du Val, New York), *pp.114/115* (Designer: Susie Ind, Pimlico Flowers, London), *pp.119* (Designer: Michael Balston; Rofford Manor, Oxfordshire)

Image Bank *p.50* (Monet's Garden)

Lucinda Lambton/Arcaid *p.45*

Andrew Lawson Front cover, *p.122*

Charles Mann *pp.76/77, p.87, pp.88, p.101, p.113*

Charles Marden Fitch Endpapers

Tania Midgley *p.82* (Belsize Park)

Clive Nichols p.5 (Designer: Anthony Noel), *p.40, p.70, p.80* (Designer: Anthony Noel), *p.102* (Designer: Anthony Noel, Fulham Park Gardens), *p.106* (Bourton House Gardens), *p.110* (Designer: Sue Berger), *pp.120/121* (Designer: Anthony Noel)

Jerry Pavia *p.100, p.107*

Harry Smith *p.15* (Hazelburg Manor), *p.24* (Walled Garden, Wisley), *pp.46/47* (Sissinghurst)

Weldon Publishing *p.73, p.83, p.85*

First published in the United Kingdom in 1993 by
ANAYA Publishers Ltd
3rd Floor, Strode House, 44-50 Osnaburgh Street
London NW1 3ND

A Kevin Weldon Production
Originally published by Weldon Publishing
a division of Kevin Weldon & Associates Pty Limited

Project Editor: Deborah Nixon
Designer: Kathie Baxter Smith
Illustrator: Valerie Price

British Library Cataloguing in Publication data

McAffer, Susan

Designing the Contained Garden—(Pleasure of Gardening Series)
I. Title II. Series
635.9

ISBN 1-85470-149-5

Designed on Quark Express in 11.5pt Garamond 3
Printed in Singapore by Kyodo Printing Co. (S'pore) Pte Ltd

Front cover: An arrangement of terracotta pots.

Back cover: Campanula latiloba.

Endpapers: Red tiles and Serjania Mexicana.

*Title page: The glorious golden-yellow flowers of a Laburnum x watereri lighten the corner and frame a sensitively placed statue
in the walled garden at Lower Hall, Worfield, England. This deciduous tree is commonly called the golden rain tree and carries
pendulous racemes of slightly scented flowers in late spring and early summer.*

*Page 4: To highlight a corner of an enclosed garden some oriental hybrid lilies have been chosen to create a spectacular display
in a massive rich blue glazed pot. Their translucent petals and strong perfume add a special quality to the night air. Two single and double
rambler roses have been used to frame the arrangement and the strap-like leaves of a flax (Phormium) add a striking accent.*

*Page 5: Terracotta pots crowded with nodding pansies add a joyful note to a window ledge in Fulham Park Gardens, London, England.
Designed by Anthony Noel.*